Introduction

Our world is a small and fragile planet, less than 8,000 miles in diameter. Nearly three-quarters of the Earth is covered by the oceans, leaving us just 29 per cent of land surface on which to live and grow most of our food.

Every minute of the day and night, some 274 babies are born around the world (395,000 babies every 24 hours). This birth rate adds another 93,000,000 people to the human population each year.

As more and more people demand more and more land for development, the wild places become smaller and fewer. The destruction of habitats means that many species of plants and animals are threatened with extinction. Poachers kill animals to meet the demands of tourists or to satisfy ancient superstitions. Pollution of the air, soil, rivers and oceans affect us all to a greater or lesser degree and the outlook can seem rather grim.

In all this gloom, there is one particular ray of hope shining through – this is the increasing interest that people like you are showing in world environmental problems. After all, it will be 'your' world before long, so you need to understand some of the problems facing the world as humanity approaches the twenty-first century. Perhaps your generation will be the first to start taking better care of Planet Earth.

Cyril Littlewood MBE, OGA
Founder & Director,
Young People's Trust for the Environment
& Nature Conservation (YPTENC)

FREE MEMBERSHIP
The Young People's Trust for the Environment & Nature Conservation (YPTENC)

If you are aged 16 or under, you can become a member of the **YPTENC** without charge and make full use of the Trust's free Information Service.

The **Information Service** can provide you with useful and informative factsheets on wildlife, endangered species and environmental problems (please include a stamped, self-addressed envelope to receive your answer).

The Trust also operates a busy **School Lecture Service** covering all age ranges and a wide variety of topics.

Another aspect of the Trust's work are the residential **Environmental Discovery Courses** for children aged 9 to 16 that it runs on the Dorset coast.

Please send for details of membership or our services to schools to:
Cyril Littlewood MBE, OGA,
Founder & Director
YPTENC, 8 Leapale Road, Guildford,
Surrey GU1 4JX
Telephone: 01483 39600
Fax: 01483 301992

Contents

The Changing World of
Deserts and Dry Lands

Our world, planet Earth, has never been still since it first formed – 4,600 million years ago. It goes around the Sun once each year, to bring the changing seasons. It spins like a top once each day, causing the cycle of day and night. Our close companion, the Moon, circles the Earth and produces the rise and fall of the ocean tides. The weather alters endlessly, too. Winds blow, water ripples into waves, clouds drift, rain falls and storms brew. Land and sea are heated daily by the Sun, and cool or freeze at night.

Living on the Earth, we notice these changes on different time scales. First and fastest is our own experience of passing time, as seconds merge into minutes and hours. We move about, eat and drink, learn and play, rest and sleep. Animals do many of these activities, too.

Second is the longer, slower time scale of months and years. Many plants grow and change over these longer time periods. Return to a natural place after many years, and you see how some of the trees have grown, while others have died and disappeared.

Third is the very long, very slow time scale lasting hundreds, thousands and millions of years. The Earth itself changes over these immense periods. New mountains thrust up as others wear down. Rivers alter their course. One sea fills with sediments, but huge earth movements and continental drift create another sea elsewhere.

The CHANGING WORLD series describes and explains these events – from the immense time span of lands and oceans, to the shorter changes among trees and flowers, to the daily lives of ourselves and other animals. Each book selects one feature or habitat of nature, to reveal in detail. Here you can read how natural DESERTS AND DRY LANDS formed, and how human activities create new ones today. You can find out how living things survive in these harsh yet exciting habitats, from spiky cacti to deadly snakes, birds of prey and, of course, camels.

MORE, AND MORE, AND ...

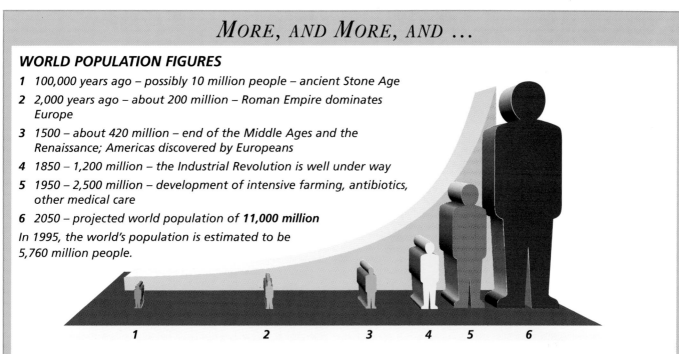

WORLD POPULATION FIGURES

1   100,000 years ago – possibly 10 million people – ancient Stone Age

2   2,000 years ago – about 200 million – Roman Empire dominates Europe

3   1500 – about 420 million – end of the Middle Ages and the Renaissance; Americas discovered by Europeans

4   1850 – 1,200 million – the Industrial Revolution is well under way

5   1950 – 2,500 million – development of intensive farming, antibiotics, other medical care

6   2050 – projected world population of **11,000 million**

In 1995, the world's population is estimated to be 5,760 million people.

The most numerous large animal on Earth, by many millions, is the human. Our numbers have increased steadily from the start of civilization about 10,000 years ago speeded by advances in public health and hygiene, the Industrial Revolution, petrol and diesel engines, better farming and better medical care.

However, this massive growth in humanity means that almost half the world's people suffer from hunger, poverty and disease. The animals and plants who share our planet also suffer. As we expand our territory, their natural areas shrink ever faster. We probably destroy one species of plant or animal every week.

However, there is another type of change affecting our world. It is the huge and ever-increasing number of humans on the planet. The CHANGING WORLD series shows how we have completely altered vast areas – to grow foods, put up homes and other buildings, mine metals and minerals, manufacture goods and gadgets from pencils to washing machines, travel in cars, trains and planes, and generally carry on with our modern lives.

This type of change is causing immense damage.

We take over natural lands and wild places, forcing plants and animals into ever smaller areas. Some of them disappear for ever. We produce all kinds of rubbish, refuse, poisons and pollution.

However, there is hope. More people are becoming aware of the problems. They want to stop the damage, to save our planet, and to plan for a brighter future. The CHANGING WORLD series shows how we can all help. We owe it to our Earth, and to its millions of plants, animals and other living things, to make a change for the better.

Lands without Water

The image that many people have of deserts is of endless sand blown by the wind and piled into tall dunes, perhaps with nomadic people in flowing robes striding across the parched landscape with their camels. But only small parts of the world's deserts are made up of sand dunes.

Deserts are the most arid, or driest, places in the world. This lack of rainfall is the main feature they have in common. In an arid area, very little rain – less than 250 millimetres – falls each year. (This compares to the rainfall for London, England, at about 600 millimetres, for New York City, USA, at 1,100 millimetres, and for Sydney in Australia at 1,180 millimetres. In a true desert, the rainfall can be much less than 250 millimetres yearly. In some deserts, such as parts of the Atacama Desert in South America, it may not rain for a hundred years!

In a desert, there is also very little other precipitation. This is the overall name for water or moisture that reaches the ground. As well as rain, it also includes snow, hail, sleet, frost and various kinds of dew. Indeed, one of the driest of all deserts

Sandy deserts
Only one-fifth of the desert areas in the world are sandy. The wind blows the loose sand into hills and ridges called dunes, which slowly change shape and creep across the landscape. This is the Sahara in North Africa, the world's biggest desert.

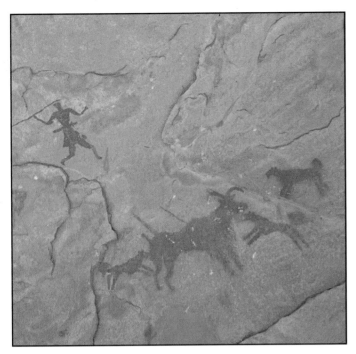

When the desert bloomed

Only a few thousand years ago, during the Stone Age, the Sahara Desert was a moist and fertile place. People lived there and grazed farm animals on lush meadows. They painted pictures of their daily life on the walls of caves. These are now hundreds of kilometres from the nearest water.

Rocky deserts

Most deserts, like the Gobi Desert of Mongolia (below), are mainly rocky. They are dry, harsh, barren plains strewn with thin soil and tough grasses. It can be bitterly cold at night and in the winter. Even colder is the Antarctic Desert (bottom). It's a desert because there is no liquid water at all. It is all frozen into ice and snow.

is on the continent of Antarctica, where all moisture falls as frozen snowflakes, and is blown away at once by strong winds, to leave bare rock. Effectively, there is no moisture at all here. This also shows that not all deserts are hot all the time. Many are scorched by day, but chilly at night. Some deserts are cold all the year round.

In hot deserts, when it does rain, the water soaks away into the ground or it is dried quickly by the hot sun or strong winds. The word 'desert' came from the words for 'an abandoned place' because no animals and plants can live without water. The small amounts of moisture in most deserts mean that some plants and animals survive there, but they must be specialists at finding and keeping water.

Deserts do not stay the same for ever. Most of the deserts in the world today formed thousands of years ago when the climate became hotter and drier after the Ice Age. Today many of the world's deserts are gradually getting larger because people are destroying the farming land around the edges and turning this to desert.

How Deserts are Made

The world's weather is driven by the Sun. As the Earth spins, and day replaces night, the Sun warms some parts of the land and the air above it more than other parts. Warmed air rises. Cooler air moves along to take its place, and we feel this moving air as wind. The Sun also warms rivers, lakes, seas and oceans, and makes water evaporate, turning it into an invisible gas called water vapour.

This vapour rises and is picked up by the wind. Its air moves over the land and blows up hills and mountains, when it expands and becomes cooler. The water vapour condenses back into water droplets, which float along in huge groups – clouds. The droplets join, get larger and become too heavy to float. They fall as rain or other precipitation.

Deserts form wherever the air has lost most of its moisture and has no rain left. There are several reasons for this. The hottest places in the world are around its middle – the Equator. Here, warm moist air rises and moves north or south as the Trade Winds. As the air rises, usually over land, it cools and drops its rain. In these

Deserts of the world
The deserts of North America, North Africa and Asia lie on the Tropic of Cancer. Those of Chile, southern Africa and Australia are on the Tropic of Capricorn. Death Valley in North America and the Patagonian Desert in South America are rain shadow deserts. The Gobi Desert is a continental desert, in the middle of the continent of Asia, thousands of kilometres from the sea.

Tropic of Cancer

Death Valley

Equator

Tropic of Capricorn

Patagonian Desert

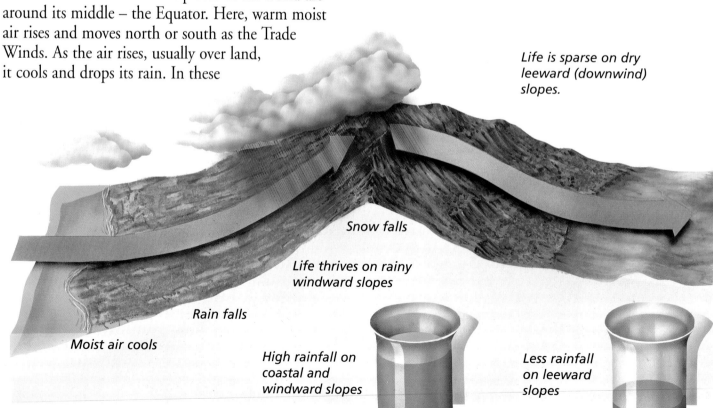

Life is sparse on dry leeward (downwind) slopes.

Snow falls

Life thrives on rainy windward slopes

Rain falls

Moist air cools

High rainfall on coastal and windward slopes

Less rainfall on leeward slopes

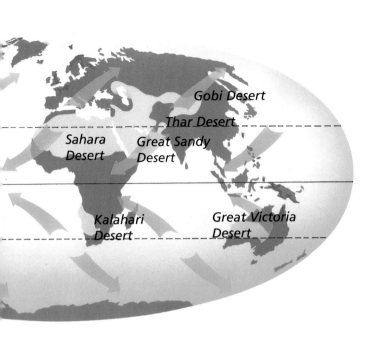

Gobi Desert

Thar Desert

Sahara Desert

Great Sandy Desert

Kalahari Desert

Great Victoria Desert

very wet places, tropical rainforests grow. The now-dry wind blows on towards the Tropic of Cancer in the north and the Tropic of Capricorn in the south. Most of the world's deserts are found in these areas, and they are tropical deserts.

Another reason why deserts form is the rain shadow effect, explained below. There are also polar deserts – vast areas of ice and snow at the North and South Poles. Any water is frozen solid, including the water inside animals which accidentally stray there, killing them at once.

The air over deserts is very dry, so there are rarely clouds in the sky. This means there is no shade from the hot sun by day. The ground gets hotter and hotter, drying any remaining water. At night there is no cloud 'blanket' to keep in the warmth of the hot ground and the hot air above it. So the ground cools very quickly, as its warmth rises high into the atmosphere. It gets colder and colder. This leads to the extremes of temperature in many deserts, with searingly hot days and shiveringly cold nights (see page 12).

Semi-desert
As the rainfall becomes less, plant life is sparse and tougher to eat. Dry scrub gives way to semi-desert. This means fewer animals live here.

Air has lost all of its water vapour (moisture).

Rain shadow desert where wind blows loose sand into dunes.

The rain shadow desert
As the wind rushes up the side of a mountain towards the peaks, it expands, cools and drops much of its moisture as rain and snow. By the time the wind blows over the other side of the mountain, it has little moisture left. So a desert forms in what is called the rain shadow area. Often, this is coupled to the continental desert effect. The farther a wind blows from the sea, the more moisture it loses. By the time it reaches the centres of the great continents, it is very dry, and deserts form.

Almost no rain in true desert.

Storms and Flash Floods

Weather happens day by day and week by week. The changing conditions of sun, wind and rain over longer time periods are known as the climate. Deserts have a dry climate. For weeks, months or even years, there is no rain.

But now and then, the weather changes. Suddenly huge dark storm clouds gather, towering kilometres into the sky. Inside the darkening clouds, water droplets are whipped up and down by powerful air currents. The water droplets rub together, causing static electricity to build up, until it must be released as a gigantic surge or spark – the lightning bolt. There is a violent flash of lightning, a clap of thunder as the lightning makes the air boil, and the cloud bursts. The water droplets grow larger until the air can hold them no longer. The storm is so violent that it releases all its pent-up energy and stored water within a few hours.

2 The cloud bursts
Perhaps 50, 100 or more millimetres of rain fall in a short time, just a few hours, usually in nearby highlands. It runs over the rocks and dry ground.

3 The gathering flood
The baked, hardened ground cannot soak up the rain. Water collects in dried river beds and surges along at amazing speed.

4 Waves of destruction
The water current sweeps away rocks, soil, plants and animals, leaving the landscape washed bare.

The flash flood
After months of drought, the parched earth is baked hard and almost waterproof. So much water hits the ground during a desert storm that it cannot soak away. It rushes over the surface, building into a fierce torrent. This effect is even more marked in rocky deserts, where there is no soil to hold the rain like a sponge.

5 Run for your life
Animals flee the area. Those sheltering in burrows are drowned.

1 Unusual weather
Rare weather conditions create a thunderstorm.

Lightning over the cactus
Lightning shoots from storm clouds over the Arizona desert. This gigantic spark heats the air around it so much that the air expands faster than the speed of sound, producing the sonic boom of thunder. In the clear air and flat landscape, a desert thunderstorm is one of Nature's most awesome displays of power.

This causes one of the most frightening features of desert life – a flash flood. The water from the sudden storm rushes along the parched gully of a wadi, or dry river bed. The water often builds up into a wall a metre or more high, surging along faster than a person can run. Everything in the flood's path is dragged along with it, including soil, sand and pebbles. Even great boulders are bounced along. Plants are torn up and washed away. Any desert animals or people who fail to reach high ground are swept along, and perhaps drowned.

For a brief time, rivers flow across the desert and pools form. The scrubby plants turn green; carpets of flowers spring from the moist ground. Puddles and lakes are alive with tadpoles and shrimps, racing to grow. But the water is only temporary. Soon it has flowed away, soaked into the ground or been dried by the sun. The drought is back.

How Hot is a Desert?

Deserts are places where temperatures are often extreme, blisteringly hot by day and unbearably cold by night. The deserts along the Tropics are the hottest. When the sun is high overhead at midday, the temperature can creep up to 40°C or more. The surface of the sand or rock is even hotter, and would burn your bare feet at once. Yet a few hours later, during the cloudless night, the temperatures plummet to 0°C or below. There may even be a frost. This pattern remains the same throughout the year. There are no proper seasons. It is summer every day, and winter every night.

The cold deserts nearer the Poles are not so hot in the day, because the sun does not rise as high in the sky. But they become even more bitingly cold at night. In the Antarctic, temperatures fall to –70°C, which is 50°C colder than a deep-freeze!

Near some coastal deserts, such as in western South America or south-west Africa, the cold water currents in the nearby sea cool the air above. This condenses its water vapour into droplets, forming fog. Almost every day the fog rolls from the sea across the sand, bringing small amounts of life-giving water to the plants and animals.

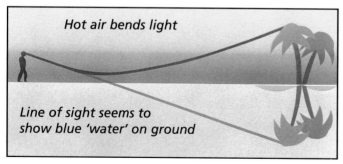

Hot air bends light

Line of sight seems to show blue 'water' on ground

Mirages
The classic mirage is a pool of blue water seen by a hot, thirsty traveller. The pool is not really there – it is a reflection of the sky above. Light is bent as it passes from the cooler air above to the extremely hot air near the ground. More complex mirages are possible.

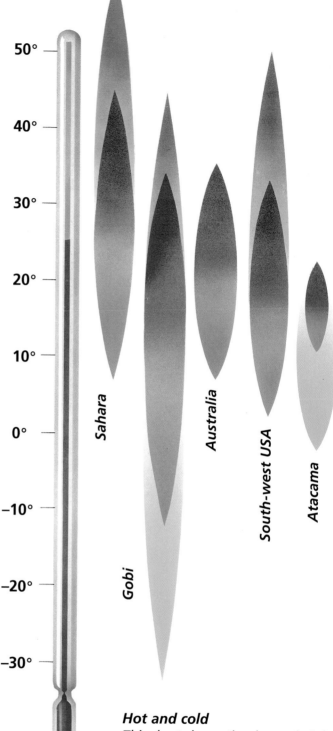

Temperature in °C (Celsius)

Hot and cold
This chart shows the day and night temperatures in various deserts. Our own body temperature is 37°C. A hot summer's day for most of us is about 30°C, while a cold wintry, windy day is around 5°C.

How Hot Does It Get?

Find out how temperatures vary according to the type of ground, rocks or sand that the Sun shines on. You need a desk lamp as the 'Sun', a 0-100°C thermometer (plastic greenhouse or outdoors version that cannot crack), separate jars containing a large rock, ordinary garden soil, clean gravel, light sand and water, also a notebook and pencil, and some gloves to avoid burning your skin.

1 Set up your equipment on a large, safe table top as shown. Adjust the lamp so that it shines down on to one of the jars, such as the jar with garden soil, from 40–50 centimetres. Put the thermometer in the soil. Measure the temperature.

2 Switch on the lamp and measure the temperature after 15 minutes. Record this in your notebook. Switch off the lamp and allow it to cool for exactly 5 minutes. Record the temperature again.

3 Test all jars in this way. Which ones warm up fastest and cool down most rapidly? Does the colour of the substance seem to make any difference? Try clear water, then water darkened with ink or food dye.

The Rain Shadow

You can make a simple rain shadow using a hosepipe and a low wall or fence. Adjust the hosepipe to a fairly wide sprinkle and aim the water at the side of the wall. What do you notice?

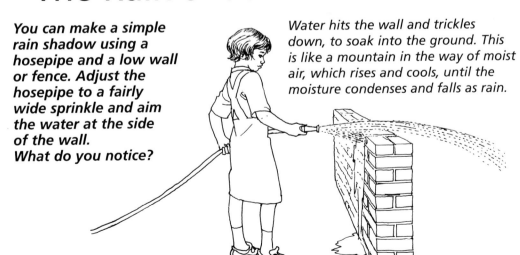

Water hits the wall and trickles down, to soak into the ground. This is like a mountain in the way of moist air, which rises and cools, until the moisture condenses and falls as rain.

The ground behind the wall is much drier, like the leeward side of a mountain. It receives less moisture because most has fallen on the other side. This is the rain shadow area. You may notice small 'rain shadow' areas around local walls, buildings and fences, where no plants grow.

Deserts of the World

Not all deserts are sandy, lifeless places. Some deserts are bare rock, or strewn with boulders or pebbles. Polar deserts are frozen, covered with ice and snow. In all but the very driest deserts, some plants and animals can survive by finding water.

In the official lists of rainfall and climate over many years, about one-third of the world's entire land area could be classed as dry. Nearly half of this dry area – about one-sixth of the world's land surface – has less than 250 millimetres of rain in an average year. This is termed 'arid'. It is mostly typical desert and very dry scrubland, with plants such as spiny cacti, spiky grasses and perhaps a few tough trees. The rest is 'semi-arid' with an average of 500 millimetres of rain every year, supporting dry scrub and shrubland, with a few clumps of trees dotted around the landscape. Only one per cent is 'extremely arid' with almost no rain at all.

Desert mountains of the Red Centre
The Macdonell Ranges are the mountains at the Red Centre of Australia. The red sand that gives the area its name is crossed by dry river beds and empty lakes. The mountains are among the most ancient on the planet. Their foundations are some 600 million years old.

There are arid and semi-arid places on every continent in the world except Europe. The west coasts of both North and South America are very dry. Most of North Africa, as well as its southern tip, is dry. Desert stretches across the whole of the Middle East and onwards to the east, across Asia. The continent with the highest proportion of dry land and desert is Australia. About four-fifths of its total area is either arid or semi-arid.

The driest and hottest places in the world lie in the centres of these arid regions. The driest of all is the Atacama Desert of Chile, South America. In some places there has been no rain at all for 400 years. The highest temperature ever recorded in the shade was 58°C in Al' Aziziyah, Libya, in the northern Sahara. In Western Australia, the temperature in Marble Bar was more than 38°C for 160 days without a break. California's Death Valley is well named – it has been even hotter, over 49°C for 43 days without a break. In these scorching conditions, the land and rocks are worn into amazing shapes by the sun and windblown sand.

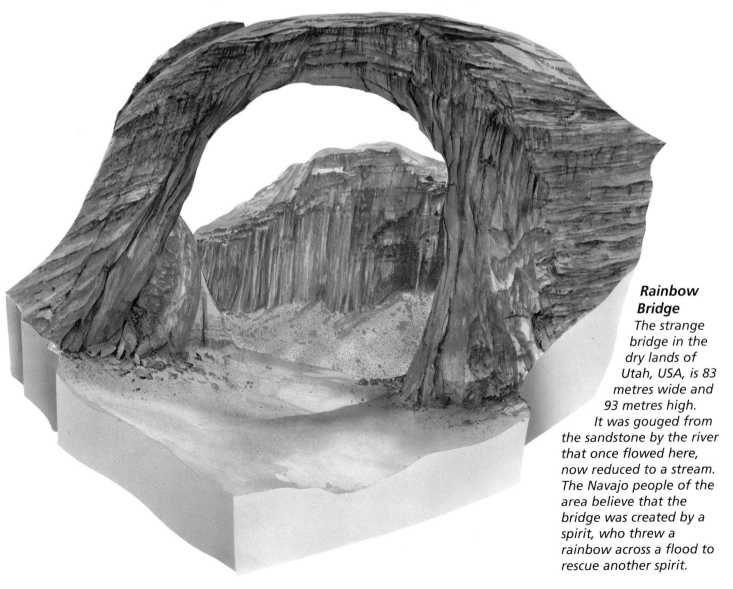

Rainbow Bridge
The strange bridge in the dry lands of Utah, USA, is 83 metres wide and 93 metres high. It was gouged from the sandstone by the river that once flowed here, now reduced to a stream. The Navajo people of the area believe that the bridge was created by a spirit, who threw a rainbow across a flood to rescue another spirit.

The Sahara Desert

Ten thousand years ago, the Sahara was a place of rivers and lakes, with a rich variety of plants and animals. But by 5,000 years ago there were only dried-up wadis (river beds) and salt flats. Today the Sahara covers 5,600,000 square kilometres of northern Africa – an area 37 times bigger than Britain, and only slightly smaller than the USA.

The word *Sahara* means 'desert' in Arabic. About one-fifth of it is sandy areas. They are called ergs – the Arabic word for a large area of sand. Most of the rest of the Sahara is gravelly or stony plains and dry valleys. In the centre there are tall mountains surrounded by rocky upland. Emi Koussi, in Chad, is the Sahara's highest mountain, at 3,415 metres above sea level.

In the north of the Sahara there are sometimes winter showers. In the south, over the Sahel (Arabic for 'desert coast'), the summer monsoons bring

Sahara Desert

Great Sand Desert

Right across Africa
The Sahara stretches from the Atlantic to the Red Sea, and from the Mediterranean south to the River Niger. It covers ten different countries. The north is mainly sand or gravel, the centre is rocky plains and mountains, and the south, the Sahel, is dry, wooded grassland.

Nomads of the Sahara
Most people who live in the desert dwell around the edges or near oases, where they can grow some crops and graze their animals. A few people also live near the oil wells and mines which tap the Sahara's rich resources. But the Tuareg people are true nomads. They travel across the desert, moving their flocks and setting up camps wherever they find water.

The sandy wastes

Few people venture into the driest, sandiest, emptiest areas, except perhaps to search for new resources of oil, gems and other mineral wealth.

downpours. But many parts of the Sahara suffer years of droughts. Often, too, violent winds blow across the desert for days on end, shaping and driving the shifting dunes and sand-blasting the rocks into fantastic sculptures. Choking, blinding sandstorms blot out the sun and engulf everything in their path.

Surprisingly, few parts of the Sahara are totally lifeless. Plants grow wherever they can find water, because the sandy soil is very fertile. Scrubby shrubs like acacia and tamarisk survive on the rock-strewn uplands, dry grasses sprout in the valleys, and palm trees flourish around pools of water, the oases. Insects, rodents and reptiles are the most common animals, but larger mammals such as gazelle are also well adapted to life here.

Camps and clothes

The camp tent lets in any breeze around its lower edges. Desert dress is also adapted to the climate, being long, loose and light. Tuareg men wear a turban, a length of fabric wound around the head, neck and face. It once disguised raiding warriors, and is still worn today – even for sleeping in.

Crossing the desert

Until 30 years ago, camel caravans with thousands of camels trailed across the Sahara, carrying goods such as silks and spices for trade in the West. Today, things have changed. Long convoys of trucks called land-trains roar along the few dusty roads that cross the desert.

Death Valley

The arid lands of North America stretch down the west coast from the Great Basin in Nevada to Chihuahua in Mexico. North of the Tropic of Cancer these are rainshadow deserts, sheltered east and west by long mountain ranges. The hottest and driest of all is Death Valley, nestled between the Panamint and Amargosa mountains in California. It is only 225 kilometres long and between 8 and 24 kilometres wide, so on a clear day you can see across it quite easily. Its lowest point is 86 metres below sea level – the lowest uncovered point of land in the Western world. A vast, sterile strip of salt flats is all that remains of a prehistoric lake. Dry river beds, called arroyos, once carried water to the valley from the mountains.

Death Valley was named for good reason. Many of the prospectors who tried to travel across it during the 1849 gold rush died on the way. The air temperature can reach an unbearable 57°C, and the ground temperature a searing 79°C. Nothing survives on the salt flats of the valley floor. But higher up the valley sides grow coarse grasses, cacti and mesquite bushes, among the sand and glistening salt crystals.

Salt in the desert
When rain falls on the mountains and snow melts, the water trickles down towards Death Valley, dissolving salts from the rocks as it goes. The water cannot escape when it reaches the low valley floor, so it forms salty lakes, or playas. These dry out to leave vast flat areas crusted with salt crystals.

Deserted desert
In the past, gold, silver, copper and borax have been mined in Death Valley, brought out by heavily laden mule trains. But today the deserted miners' settlements stand as landmarks on the modern tourist trail.

The Gobi Desert

The Gobi Desert lies mainly across Mongolia and northern China. It covers an area of 1,295,000 square kilometres, nearly nine times larger than Great Britain. The desert's name comes from the Mongolian word for 'a place without water'. There are fewer people living here, in terms of land area, than almost anywhere else in the world, except for the highest mountain ranges.

Most of the Gobi is about 900 metres above sea level. The Altai Mountains to the north-west rise another 3,000 metres. It is a place of rock, coarse gravel and salty sand, crossed by dry river beds which end disappointingly as salt flats. There is little soil. Only scattered clumps of tough grass and goosefoot, and bushes of sage and tamarisk, can find a root-hold. But this vegetation supports scattered herds of wild asses and gazelles, and smaller creatures find cover among the matted stems and in burrows beneath, among the tangled roots. Groups of nomadic peoples wander to find grazing for their camels, goats, sheep and ponies.

The eastern end of the Gobi Desert has about 200 millimetres of rain each year. But the western end, several thousand kilometres from the sea, has less than half this amount. As in most deserts, the temperatures rise sharply by day and fall rapidly by night. But the seasonal changes in the Gobi are very dramatic, too. In July the temperature soars to 50°C, but in wintry January it can be as low as

DINOSAUR DESERT

About 150 million years ago, part of the Gobi Desert was covered by a sea. As it began to dry out into a patchwork of lakes, marshes and drier areas, it became an ideal place for the most successful reptiles ever – the dinosaurs. Chinese people have been using fossilized dinosaur bones as traditional medicines for thousands of years.

In 1922, a USA-led team of scientists went into the Gobi to discover the source of these relics. Despite the appalling conditions, they brought back some of the most spectacular fossil finds in the world, including the first fossil dinosaur eggs ever discovered. Recent expeditions have also made exciting finds of new dinosaur species.

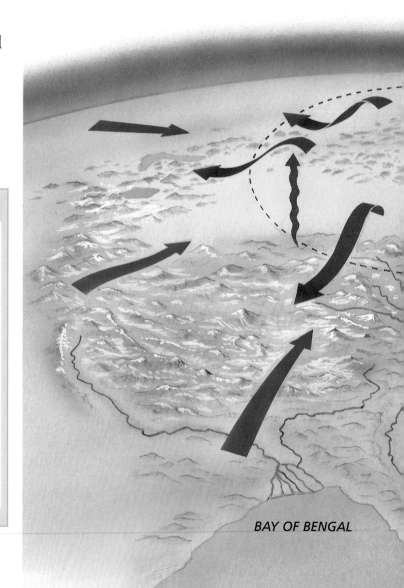

BAY OF BENGAL

–40°C. These temperature differences cause ferocious winds that blow the sand and dust about, adding to the drying effect, coating the land and suffocating plants and animals in choking clouds.

Like other deserts, the Gobi has not always been dry. Fossils show that moisture-loving plants and animals lived there millions of years ago. As the area dried out, many types of dinosaurs made it their home. They included the egg-eating *Oviraptor*, the ostrich-like *Gallimimus*, the pig-sized *Protoceratops* with its nests and eggs, the 'speedy thief' called *Velociraptor*, and the massive, meat-eating *Tarbosaurus*. In fact, stony deserts are excellent places for finding all kinds of fossils, since there is little soil cover to hide the rocks, and the Sun's heat cracks and flakes the surface, continually exposing new finds. The hot, dry, bare 'Badlands' of the USA have also yielded some of the best fossils of prehistoric beasts and plants.

The continental desert
The moist winds (blue arrows) from the sea drop their water as rain, as they blow over the first patches of land. By the time a wind reaches the centre of a great land mass, it has lost all its moisture. The Gobi Desert has formed mainly in this manner, and so it is a continental desert.

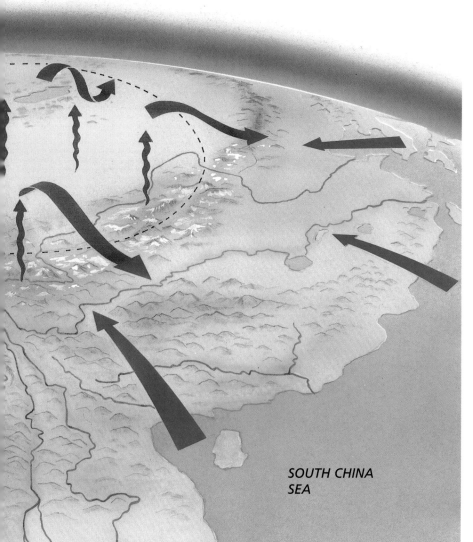

SOUTH CHINA SEA

Australian deserts
The dry outback and deserts of Australia stretch across the centre of the continent to the western coasts (see page 22).
In the south is the Great Victoria Desert. In the mid-west is the Gibson Desert, and to the north-west, the Great Sandy Desert. In the central regions, many sand dunes are 'live', moved by the wind. Elsewhere they are 'fixed' by the thin, tough mat of plants.

Southern Deserts

In South America, the deserts of Peru and Chile lie along the coast of the Pacific Ocean, in the rain shadow of the Andes Mountains. The area is not hot, but it is dry and littered with salt basins. Its main moisture comes off the sea as fog. Farther south in Patagonia it is even colder. Strong, drying winds, called pamperos, blow much of the time.

In southern Africa, the Namib Desert is one of the oldest deserts in the world. Gravel beds littered with gemstones nestle between the sand dunes. Almost no rain falls here, but every few days, fog rolls in from the sea. The animals and plants have adapted to use this source of water to survive. The Kalahari Desert to the east was once covered by an inland sea, which is now reduced to the swamps of the Okavango.

Bushmen of the Kalahari
The people who live in the Kalahari Desert are called San Bushmen. Until recently, they got everything they needed from the desert by hunting and foraging. But like many desert peoples, some of them have adopted the customs and lifestyles of the Western world.

Namib Desert
One of the oldest deserts in the world, it has sand dunes that roll down almost to the shores of the Atlantic. Only a few wandering Bushmen live here.

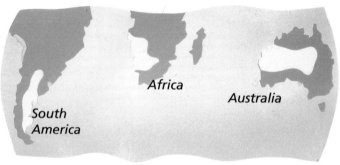

South America

Africa

Australia

Australia's vast deserts (see page 21) are dry for two reasons. They lie on the Tropic of Capricorn, so they are hot from the tropical effect. They are at the centre of a huge landmass, so they are dry from the continental effect. Australia also has mountain ranges whose rainshadow areas add to the dryness.

Sometimes it does not rain in the central desert regions for years, and then suddenly enough falls to form great lakes. Mulga and mallee bushes, types of acacia, grow in the driest parts of the outback and provide food for the unique Australian wildlife.

Salt And More Salt

Some dry areas have salt pans and salt flats. Rain falls far away and soaks along through the ground, dissolving soil salts and minerals as it goes. In the dry area it rises to the surface and evaporates, leaving the salts behind. Almost nothing can live in the parched, corrosive salt pan.

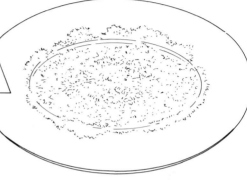

3 Let the water evaporate, or speed up the process with a desk lamp. Glinting crystals of salt are left, like a miniature salt pan.

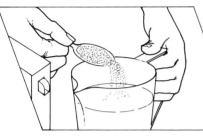

1 Add 5 tablespoons of table salt to one litre of water, and stir to dissolve it. See how the salt crystals 'disappear', like soil minerals dissolving in groundwater.

2 Pour the clear, normal-looking water into a dark saucer or a clear glass or plastic dish on dark card. This is the salt-rich soil water.

How A Desert Forms

As rainfall gets less and moisture becomes scarce, life is harder. If you have a patch of garden or similar land, you can make your own desert – simply by making it dry.

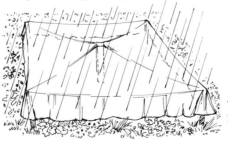

1 Choose a patch of ground about 2 metres square. It should be flat and look healthy, with plenty of plants. Identify and record the plants.

2 Push in some sticks around the patch and fix a large plastic sheet over it about 50 cm off the ground. Put a taller stick in the centre so that rain does not puddle in the middle.

3 Each week, examine the central area under the sheet and record your results. Sunlight and wind can get here, but not moisture. After a few months, the plants have withered and died. You have made a 'desert'.

How Deserts Form

In most places in the world, the landscape is constantly being smoothed down and moved around by the weather. The cracking and rubbing effects of heat, cold, wind, rain and frost – called erosion – gradually wear mountain peaks down to smooth hills and fill up valleys with the resulting particles. But the desert is different. Nothing happens gradually or smoothly. Everything happens suddenly, unexpectedly and with great ferocity.

All kinds of bedrock are found in deserts. The ancient Egyptians cut blocks of granite, one of the hardest of all rocks, to make the stone coffins of their pharaohs. Deserts that were once oceans, like the Gobi, consist of softer rocks such as sandstone.

The bedrock is cracked by frost or hot sun, but the broken bits may stay where they are for months, until there are strong winds or a flash flood (see page 10). Over the higher parts of a desert, and on the slopes of the surrounding mountains or a raised central plateau, the wind and occasional rain will crack and strip the underlying rock bare, leaving sharp angular shapes.

New angular sand grain

Shaped sand fragments
As the fragments of rock, gravel and sand are rolled and blown about, they wear down into smaller and smaller particles. The corners rub off and they become rounded.

Corners wear away

Old rounded sand grain

Desert soil
Fertile soil forms only where bits of dead plants and animals collect and rot. This makes humus which can absorb moisture and provide nourishment for the new growth of plants, and the animals that feed on them. Otherwise, the sand is lifeless.

Thin surface soil

Sandy subsoil

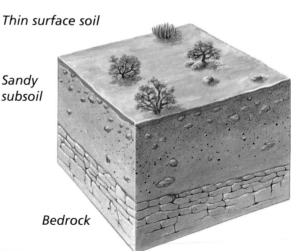

Bedrock

The bedrock is chipped into gravel when flash floods hurl pebbles at the rock, or when the evening dew seeps into cracks and then freezes at night, expanding and cracking the rock. Sometimes the rain water contains acids which dissolve the rock. Sometimes the dust-laden wind sandblasts chunks from it. The pieces of rock and gravel are eventually worn down to sand particles. These are small enough to be carried by the wind.

As the wind blows over the dunes and hills of the desert, it carries different-sized particles for different distances, sorting them and forming strange shapes. The finer and lighter the sand particles, the farther the wind blows them. The faster the wind blows, the larger the particles it can carry.

How the wind makes dunes

When the wind blows up the long slope of a sand dune, its speed increases slightly and it whips the sand over the top. Here it slows down and drops the larger sand particles.

Wind-shaped wonders

The wind picks up grains and blows them against the rocks. Softer rocks are sandblasted more easily than harder rocks, producing wonderful natural sculptures.

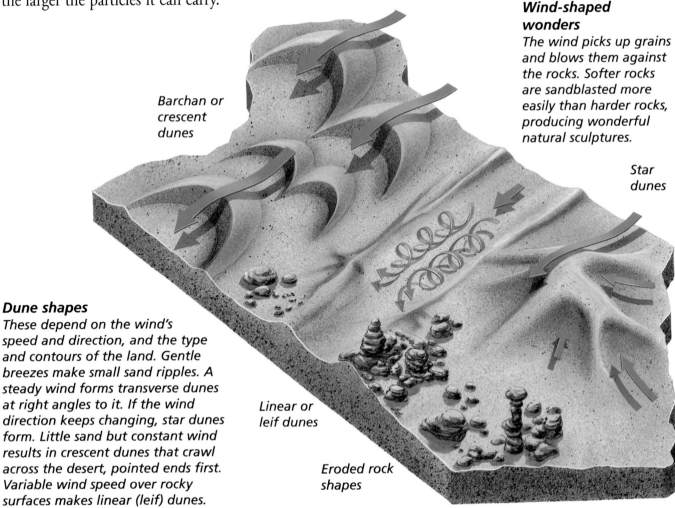

Barchan or crescent dunes

Star dunes

Linear or leif dunes

Eroded rock shapes

Dune shapes

These depend on the wind's speed and direction, and the type and contours of the land. Gentle breezes make small sand ripples. A steady wind forms transverse dunes at right angles to it. If the wind direction keeps changing, star dunes form. Little sand but constant wind results in crescent dunes that crawl across the desert, pointed ends first. Variable wind speed over rocky surfaces makes linear (leif) dunes.

Oasis!

Surprisingly, there is water in the driest of deserts, but it is deep under the ground. The underground water is called groundwater. It falls perhaps hundreds of kilometres away, as rain, and seeps through the tiny holes in porous or spongy rock. This groundwater dribbles slowly down and along, through layers of porous rock, until it reaches the deep level where the rocks are full of water. This is the water table, and the water-soaked rocks are called aquifers.

In most parts of the desert, the water table is dozens of metres below the ground. But here and there, the land dips down to meet it. The groundwater wells up to form a desert spring, perhaps a stream, and a small pool – an oasis.

Desert oases are islands of life in the sea of drought. Leafy plants grow in abundance.

Small oases are used by people and their animals as stopping places for food and water. Whole towns have grown up around larger oases. The people channel or carry the water to their fields and grow crops, especially dates from date palms – trees that thrive in such conditions.

The underground water store is vast, but not limitless, and it has taken many thousands of years to collect. Where people make artificial oases, by sinking wells and pumping the water into their irrigation ditches, they use it hundreds of times faster than it can be replaced.

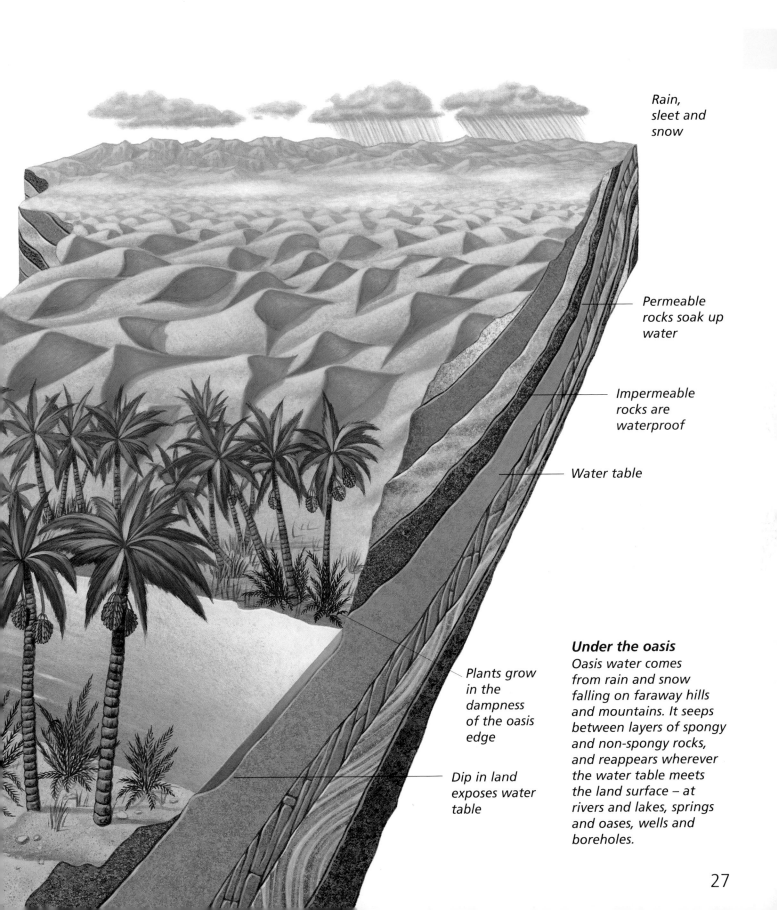

Rain, sleet and snow

Permeable rocks soak up water

Impermeable rocks are waterproof

Water table

Plants grow in the dampness of the oasis edge

Dip in land exposes water table

Under the oasis
Oasis water comes from rain and snow falling on faraway hills and mountains. It seeps between layers of spongy and non-spongy rocks, and reappears wherever the water table meets the land surface – at rivers and lakes, springs and oases, wells and boreholes.

27

River in the Desert

There are two kinds of rivers found in deserts –
permanent and temporary. Permanent rivers rise
in mountains far from the desert, so they always
have a water supply. They flow across the desert
to the sea. Only the largest of the world's rivers
carry sufficient water to cross deserts without
soaking away or drying up. They include the
River Nile in Egypt, the Niger in West Africa
and the Colorado in the USA.

Egypt's ancient lifeline
*The River Nile flows
along the eastern edge
of the Sahara Desert. In
ancient times, every year
its waters rose and left
fertile black mud along
its banks. These narrow
strips of farmland
nurtured the Ancient
Egyptian civilization for
thousands of years. Today
the water is controlled by
dams and irrigation
channels, so the seasonal
flood is much smaller.*

Temporary rivers and streams flow only after
downpours. The water rushes along channels that
are normally dry. These channels are called wadis in
Africa and Asia, and arroyos in parts of the
Americas. The river ends where the water finally
soaks away into the ground or into a salty mud flat,
or forms a short-lived lake. Before the desert
climate developed, thousands of years ago, many of
these now-dry river beds were major rivers flowing
to the sea. Today, their only water is deep in the
ground. Here and there, the land dips down to this
water, making small pools or lakes in the river bed.

Major waterway
The River Nile is used for communication and transport by traditional ships and boats, and for sightseeing by modern tourist craft. In places, the dry desert almost touches its banks.

Making New Deserts

Life for desert people has always been difficult. But people such as the San Bushmen of the Kalahari and the Aboriginals of Australia have managed to survive by knowing where to find food and water, and taking only what they needed, leaving the rest for another time. Most desert people live around the edges of the arid lands.

Today, the world has more and more people and more of them are trying to exist on desert edges. Farmers cut down the slow-growing, stunted trees for firewood, and graze their animals on the fragile plants. Some clear the land to grow crops, but the climate is usually far too dry. The crops soon use up all of the soil's goodness. Wells are dug to irrigate the fields, but this uses water thousands of times faster than it collects.

As the water table falls, the water becomes poisonous with salts and other chemicals, or the wells run dry. The end result is usually the same.

The crops die and their roots shrivel, no longer holding the parched soil together. It turns to dust and blows away, leaving another patch of desert. This type of disaster happened in the USA in the 1930s, known as the Dustbowl. In its most severe form it is called 'desertification', and it still happens today all around the world, but especially in Africa.

The US Dustbowl
In the 1900s, farmers ploughed the USA's natural dry prairies and planted vast fields of wheat and other farm plants. Many years of crops sapped the soil's goodness (centre right). In the 1930s, a long drought killed the plants and their roots shrivelled. The soils, loose and unprotected, blew away in great dust storms that buried entire houses and coated the land with fine dust (upper right). The land took years to recover and many farmers had no work (lower right).

GOATS

Goats are ideal domestic animals for arid regions. They can eat almost anything, go for long periods without water, and provide wool, milk and meat. But where there are too many goats, they kill the plants and lay the soil bare. They even climb into trees to eat the bark and leaves.

The Well of Life

You can show how a desert well or oasis works, with this model version. You need an old sponge, some sand, a large plastic tank such as an aquarium, modelling clay, a drinking straw and water.

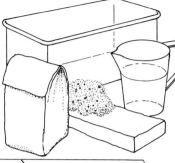

1 Put sand in the tank, heaped at the sides to make a valley shape. Flatten the clay into a sheet and put this over the sand in a wide U shape. Make a small hole in the lowest part of the clay. Insert the straw so it pokes in the sand below.

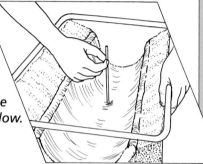

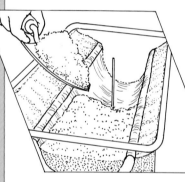

2 Add more sand on the clay, to make the middle valley flat. Cut off the straw just above sand level, which should be below the level of the sand at the sides.

3 Pour water on to the sand at the sides. This is a rain-soaked hill. The water soaks into the sand, and is trapped by the impervious clay. Add more water, and the level of the water table rises. Finally water comes up the straw, which is a miniature well or oasis.

Table-top Sand Dunes

This project blows things around, so do it out of doors on a calm day, where a small mess will not matter. You need a large table, some fine sand (or you could use table salt or sugar) in a shallow tray, and a hair-drier or a vacuum cleaner set to 'blow'.

1 Pile sand in the middle of the table. Blow it with the hair-drier, adjusting the drier's distance and power so that it moves sand grains without blowing them away.

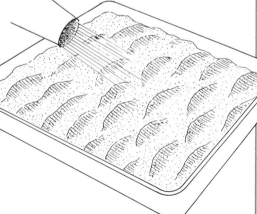

2 Blow down at the sand. Or blow along and low down. See how tiny dunes form. Move the drier around to represent a variable wind. Do the dunes change their shape?

Plants of the Desert

Life in the desert is harsh – especially for plants. Unlike animals, they cannot move around to find water. Rooted to the spot, they have to cope with drought, thin poor soil, sandstorms, extremes of temperature and many other problems.

Plants need three essentials to survive: sunlight, nutrients in the soil and water. A plant makes its food and gets the energy to live and grow by capturing the energy in sunlight, using a chemical process called photosynthesis. This usually takes place in the leaves. In the desert, there is rarely a shortage of sunlight, but finding water is much more difficult. As moisture evaporates from a plant's leaves, it draws more water from the ground into its roots, to replace the lost moisture. Many desert plants have special features to cope with drought. They find water with deep or widespread roots, store as much as possible inside swollen leaves or stems, and cut down moisture loss in many ways.

Prince's plume
The silvery leaves of this dry-land flower are covered in tiny hairs. This helps to cut down water loss, since the hairs trap air and water vapour close to the leaf surface.

Wild carrot
Like its farmed relation, the wild carrot has a thickened main root, or tap root. But in the wild version, this is whitish rather than orange, and woody, which helps it to withstand drought and loose soil. Wild carrots grow in many dry places such as chalky soils and grassy banks.

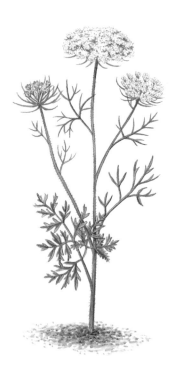

Cacti: A Success Story

The most successful desert plants are the cacti. They grow mostly in the arid lands of the Americas, although they have also become popular pot-plants all over the world. The Mexican prickly pear cactus has spread itself so successfully, being introduced to new regions, that it is a pest or weed in many countries, especially Australia. Cacti belong to the large plant group called 'succulents'. All succulents can store water in their leaves, stems or roots.

Most cacti are stem succulents, storing moisture in their barrel-like stems. In fact, all parts of a typical cactus have adapted to help the plant endure the harshest conditions. Most plants lose much water from their leaves. Cacti have lost their leaves. In a cactus, the leaf's main job of making food from sunlight has been taken over by the stem. This is green in colour, like a leaf. It also has a thick, waxy covering, so that very little of the water stored inside it can pass through and be lost into the air.

HOW PLANTS FIND WATER

Some desert plants have one long tap root that goes straight down to the water table. The mesquite bush's tap root may be 30 metres long. Others have a fine network of roots that spread far and wide, just under the surface, to cover a great area and soak up rainwater when it comes. A few plants of arid areas, like the pygmy cedar tree, can soak up the moisture of dew or mist droplets through their leaves.

The roots of the bishop's hat cactus can grow through stony, dry soil to reach water below.

Notocactus *from South America is a ribbed globular shape with long, sharp spines.*

Lobivia *from South America is a clustering cactus with soft, pale spines.*

The bishop's hat cactus has a globular body with large ribs. It comes from Mexico.

Saguaro or Carnegia *cacti* grow as tall as trees.

Cereus cacti are tall and branching, with ribs and spines.

Euphorbias are succulents but not not true cacti. They have similar adaptations to desert life.

Opuntia, or prickly pear, is a segmented cactus with flat discs.

The rat's tail cactus from Mexico has slender creeping stems.

Cacti usually flower after rain, when insects are also breeding.

Cactus shape and size
Many cacti are barrel-shaped, but there is a huge variety in shape and size. The famous saguaro cactus with its arm-like side branches may grow 15 metres tall and weigh 10 tonnes. Birds perch on it and peck nesting holes in it. But most cacti are small and grow low and slow.

The stem of a cactus is a living water butt. It is usually covered with spines as protection against hungry, thirsty animals. The covering is folded like a concertina so that the spongy, succulent flesh inside can swell as it soaks up water during damp times. The water comes into the stem through the roots. Some cacti have fine roots that cover a large area, others have long tap roots that go down deep.

Most cacti grow very slowly and can live to a great age. The globose cacti of Mexico may be a thousand years old! There are a few giants, as big as trees, but most are smaller than your fist. Cacti flower rarely, usually only after rain. They produce bright, showy blooms to attract insects, which spread their pollen and help them to set seed.

Are They Dead?

Cacti can endure the desert drought and dryness, surviving on the water stored in their stems. But other desert plants seem to give up and die during the harshest times. However, they are usually not quite dead. They are 'dormant', in a kind of deep sleep, waiting for better times.

These plants shut down nearly all of their life processes. Their leaves die and fall. Some even appear to shed their stems and most of their roots, too. Others exist only as underground parts, with no trace on the surface. But they cling to life, often for years, and they are ready to reawaken and start growing again when the rains come. A parched desert may look lifeless, but underground, dormant plants are crowded together in their thousands.

Plants that stay above the ground are often deciduous. This means that they lose their leaves, like common woodland trees such as oaks, ashes and beeches. But the desert plants do not shed their leaves in autumn. They shed them as the damp spell draws to a close, and the desert becomes

Fire-thorn
Also known as the ocotillo, this bush produces fiery red flowers. It also withstands bush fires well and is one of the first plants to begin growing again after the flames have passed.

Trees in dry lands
Some trees, including acacias, survive in dry grassland, scrub and semi-desert. They are called wattles in Australia and thorn-trees in Africa. Many have spines for protection against browsing animals. Ants burrow into the spine bases and set up home in the resulting galls (see page 42).

dry again. During parched times, these plants appear leafless and lifeless. The American ocotillo or fire-thorn loses all of its leaves. The quiver tree, a kind of African tree-aloe, sheds clumps of leaves from the ends of its branches. The Mexican brittlebush even drops whole branches. These plants cannot grow until their leaves sprout again from buds, when it rains. Then the leaves can catch the energy in sunlight and let the plant grow again. Some plants, like the resurrection plant, keep their leaves, but they turn from green to brown and shrivel in the dry heat. They can remain like this for months or years. As soon as it rains, the leaves swell and turn green within a few days. Plants that do this are called 'xerophytes'. They get a quicker start than plants which grow new leaves from buds.

Two leaves only

The Welwitschia *from the arid regions of southern and south-western Africa is one of the world's strangest plants. It has only two trailing, strap-shaped leaves which grow up to 6 metres long. It gets nearly all its moisture from fog and dew (see page 43).*

Quiver tree

This African tree sheds clumps of leaves during the dry periods.

Huge reserves

The elephant's foot yam can store huge supplies of water and nutrients in its underground parts.

UNDERGROUND LIFE

In a tropical forest, the plant biomass (weight of plant material) above the ground may be more than 100 kilograms (kg) per square metre. In a desert, the above-ground plant biomass might be less than 5 kg per square metre. But hidden below the surface could be another 25 kg of roots, tubers (fat underground stems), corms and bulbs.

The Desert Garden

Look through a good gardening book to find advice on growing plants in dry places in the garden. These are suited to a desert garden. Some books have special information on growing cacti in pots, where you can limit the amount of watering to copy desert conditions.

Hold and move cacti with bent strips of soft card. This prevents damage to them and your fingers!

Check that all the varieties you wish to grow like similar conditions of light, temperature and moisture.

Put larger specimens at the back, smaller ones near the front.

Cover the pot compost with sand or small pebbles, so it looks like a real desert.

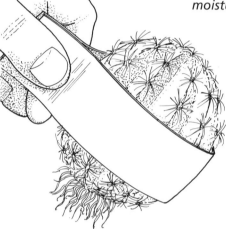

Put a few drops of liquid fertilizer in the water occasionally, to ensure the plants have enough minerals.

How Fast Do They Grow?

Grow some seeds of fast-growing summer flowers. Put them in four similar pots on the same window-sill, so they all get the same sunlight and temperature. But set up and treat the pots differently. Which seeds grow best?

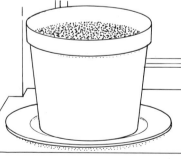

1 Fill with good-quality soil, watered regularly so it is moist (but not soggy or wet).

2 Fill with clean sand, watered regularly so it is moist (but not soggy or wet).

Take care: do not give the plants too much water. In the desert, it may rain on only a few days each year.

3 Good-quality soil, hardly watered at all, so it is very dry.

4 Sand, hardly watered at all, so it is very dry.

Compare Rainfalls

Plant life gives clues to rainfall. See how rainfall varies even around a local garden, park or field, by making rain gauges. You need several plastic soft-drinks bottles, a notebook and a pencil.

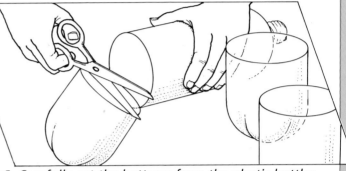

1 Carefully cut the bottoms from the plastic bottles, making cup shapes about 15 centimetres tall.

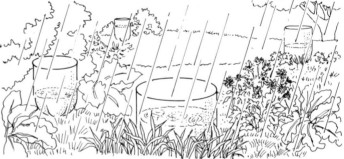

2 When rain is forecast, place the rain gauges in various places around the garden or park. Put some out in the open. Place others where few plants grow and the soil is bare, such as near walls or fences.

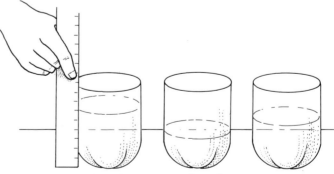

3 Straight after the rain, gather the gauges. Compare their levels. Can you work out why some have collected more rain than others? Try to link this to the moisture in the ground, and how many plants grow there.

After the Rain

One way of avoiding the driest desert conditions is to produce seeds as quickly as possible when there has been rain. Inside a seed's tough, waterproof coat, the tiny embryo (baby) plant can survive the driest conditions until the rain brings it back to life. This means that, only days after rain, the dry desert becomes a carpet of vibrant colours. The tiny seeds lying in the sand have germinated, grown fragile roots, stems and leaves, and produced glorious flowers. The blooms attract insects to carry the pollen from flower to flower. But soon the plants wither in the scorching sun and the desert colours return to yellow sand and brown rocks.

Plants which grow, flower quickly and die like this, whenever conditions are right, are called 'ephemerals'. Their seeds respond to certain changes in conditions. Some are coated in chemicals which prevent their growth, until washed off by water. Other seeds have tough coats that only crack and allow growth when hurled along in a flash flood.

The desert in bloom

In the Kalahari Desert of south-west Africa, carpets of brightly coloured flowers stretch far into the distance – only days after a desert rainstorm. In a few more days, these delicate plants will have shed their seeds and be withered and brown. The seeds may have to wait years for the next rain.

SEED DISPERSAL

Desert plants need to spread their seeds as far as possible, to reach new places for growth. Daisy seeds have tiny parachutes to blow in the wind. Some cactus fruits are eaten by animals. The seeds pass through the animal's gut and emerge in a lump of manure, ready planted and fertilized! After American tumbleweed dies, the wind breaks it from its shrivelled roots and blows it across the dry land. As it rolls, it spills out its seeds.

41

Disguise and Defence

Apart from the hazards of the fierce desert heat and dryness, plants face other dangers. Animals in the desert are desperate for water and food – and plants can provide both. So different plants have different ways of defending or disguising themselves, to avoid being eaten or damaged. Some are disguised as inedible things. The fleshy leaves of living stone plants look just like pebbles. Most of the plant is below ground, hidden from the Sun's heat and the night's cold, and out of sight of hungry animals. The smoothly rounded leaf tips are a perfect match for the real pebbles around the plant, no matter what colour they are. The living stone can mimic the blue-greys of slate, the browns and yellows of sandstone, and even the gleaming white of quartz.

Another option is defence. Cacti (see page 34) are famous for their ferocious spines. So too are many other desert plants like aloes and agaves. The

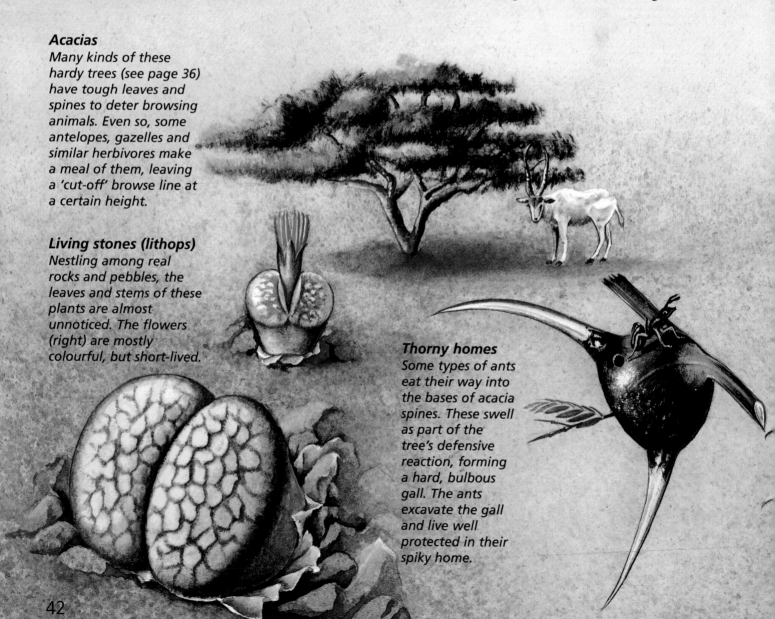

Acacias
Many kinds of these hardy trees (see page 36) have tough leaves and spines to deter browsing animals. Even so, some antelopes, gazelles and similar herbivores make a meal of them, leaving a 'cut-off' browse line at a certain height.

Living stones (lithops)
Nestling among real rocks and pebbles, the leaves and stems of these plants are almost unnoticed. The flowers (right) are mostly colourful, but short-lived.

Thorny homes
Some types of ants eat their way into the bases of acacia spines. These swell as part of the tree's defensive reaction, forming a hard, bulbous gall. The ants excavate the gall and live well protected in their spiky home.

tiny leaves and trumpet flowers of a Middle Eastern convolvulus (bindweed) grow between spines several centimetres long. The Saharan thornbush is named for its method of defence. The famous spinifex grass of the Australian desert has tough leaves with sharp edges and spines on the end. Few animals eat them. But many, like the spinifex hopping mouse, use these spiny clumps as well-protected homes.

Other plants use chemical defences. The creosote bush grows in the hot, dry areas of the south-western USA and Mexico. Its waxy leaves contain poisonous scented oils, whose smell give this plant its name. The bush grows to about 3 metres in height and very few creatures can eat the leaves – although the creosote-bush grasshopper lives nowhere else. The bush's branches bend over and grow their own roots into the ground, so the plant spreads outwards in an ever widening ring. Some creosote bushes have gone on growing for more than 10,000 years. Members of the onion family which grow in the desert are also avoided by most animals because of their eye-stinging sap.

Hooked spines
The ferocactus has a small round stem bearing very long hairs and spines, some of which are hooked. But most of the plant is below the ground. It consists of a very long, fleshy tap root that may weigh ten times as much as the stem visible above.

WATER FROM THE AIR

Many desert plants can absorb moisture from the air around them in the form of water vapour. This moisture may settle as dew or be blown along as mist or fog, especially over deserts near the sea. In the Namib Desert of south-western Africa, the early morning mist leaves beads of dew on bushy lichens that grow on the rocks, on the long twisted and shredded leaves of *Welwitschia* (see page 37) and on the salt-encrusted tips of the saltbush. This moisture is quickly sucked in by the plant's tissues, enabling them to live another day.

Desert Plant-eaters

Like desert plants, desert animals also have to cope with burning heat and lack of water. But they have the advantage over plants, of being able to move to a more comfortable place. Animals that eat plants are called herbivores. In the desert there are very few plants and they are often protected by spines or poisons, or are difficult to find. The dry, woody plants are not very nutritious and are tough to digest. Some desert browsers, like goats and camels, can crunch the waxy leaves and spines. But most animals prefer the more nutritious seeds and stems, or the roots swollen with stored water.

Desert animals use their water carefully. They hardly sweat and they produce very concentrated liquid waste (urine) and dry, or even powdery, droppings (faeces). Desert reptiles such as snakes and lizards produce thick, pasty waste matter.

Small animals avoid the heat by finding shade during the hottest parts of the day. Many live in burrows where the air stays cool and moist, and only come out at night to find food. Some even

JUST THE OCCASIONAL DRINK

Precious water
Smaller plant-eaters, like gerbils, can exist on the water they find in their food. They hardly ever need to drink. Larger desert beasts such as wild asses store water in their body tissues. They need to drink only once every several days, when the stores are used up, but then they take in huge amounts at one session.

Solid wastes
Most desert creatures produce very dry body wastes, so they do not lose valuable water in their droppings.

go into a type of deep sleep, called 'aestivation', during the hottest and driest parts of the year.

The camel has long been famous as the 'ship of the desert', carrying goods across a sea of sand dunes. This animal is ideally suited for long desert journeys, able to walk 160 kilometres in one day. It can digest tough plants, go for days without water, endure high body temperatures without harm, and close its eyes and nostrils against sandstorms. Its round, flat feet are like sand-shoes and do not sink into soft ground. The short, coarse fur and fatty hump insulate the body from the hot sun and cold night air. The fat stored in the hump can be turned into food. A thirsty camel may drink 100 litres of water in a few minutes, and store some of this in its stomach for days. Camels were taken to the desert regions of Australia, as beasts of burden. Some escaped and now live semi-wild in the dry outback.

One hump or two?
Bactrian camels come from Asia and have two humps. Most are domesticated, belonging to Mongolian herders. A few are still wild. But all dromedaries, or one-humped camels, are (or were) domesticated. In Africa they are used for carrying goods, for racing, for milk and meat and hides, and for traditional ceremonies.

45

Dry Land Insects

The desert is home to many small crawling creatures. Few are out and about in the burning heat of the day. Most are hiding under stones, in cracks or buried in the sand or soil. They emerge in the coolness of dusk, to search for food and a mate during the night. Insects have a hard, waxy waterproof outer case to their bodies, so they do not dry out. Most insects also have long legs to keep their bodies off the hot sand or rocks. Many can fly in the cooler air above the ground.

Some insects, such as butterflies, do not see out the driest times. They breed and leave offspring in the form of eggs or pupae (chrysalises), which are better able to survive drought. After rain, the adult butterflies emerge to sip sugary nectar from the ephemeral flowers and lay their eggs. The eggs hatch when the next rains come, and the caterpillars feed hungrily on the leaves of the next generation of plants. They turn into pupae as quickly as possible.

Many insects store food during times of plenty, for future times of scarcity. Honey-pot ants keep

The darkening sky
Locusts live alone, like other desert grasshoppers, for most of the time. But after several rainy seasons, when food is plentiful, their numbers build up. The young wingless 'hoppers' gather, grow fully and fly off in huge swarms of millions, in search of food.

Darkling Beetle
These beetles drink from the morning mist.

Sun-spider
This desert hunter is not a true spider but a relative of spiders and scorpions. It poisons and devours its prey.

Dung beetles
Nothing is wasted in the desert. Any source of nourishment is food for something. Dung beetles roll the droppings of larger animals into balls, lay their eggs in them and bury them in pits. The grubs hatch out into a tasty lump of food.

Giant desert mite
The giant desert mite is about the size of a housefly, has a red velvety covering, and eats any scraps it can find.

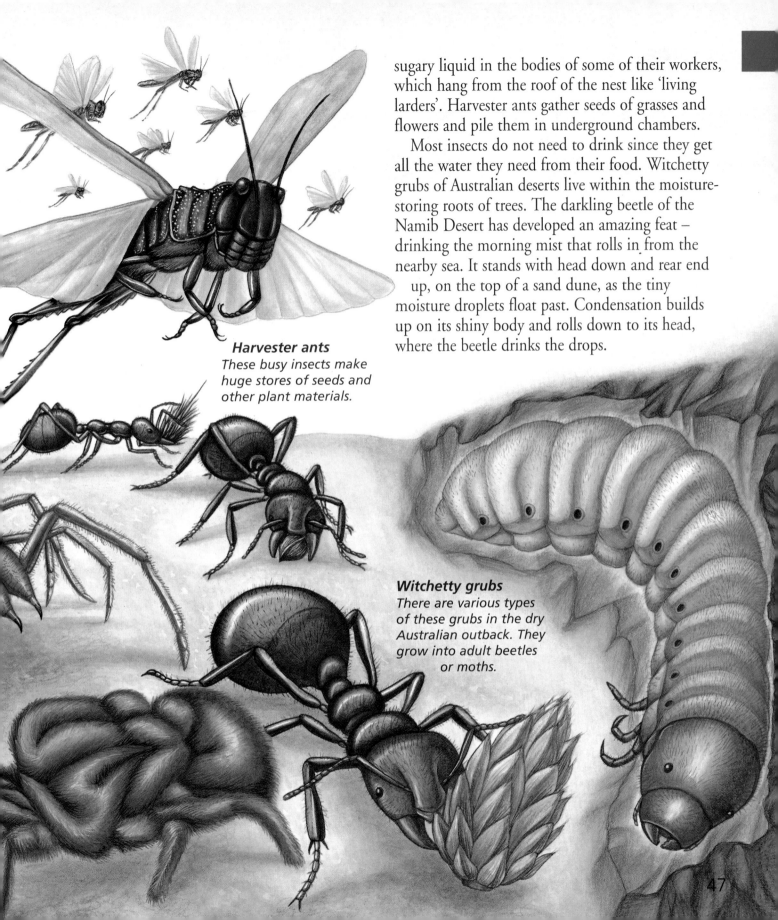

sugary liquid in the bodies of some of their workers, which hang from the roof of the nest like 'living larders'. Harvester ants gather seeds of grasses and flowers and pile them in underground chambers.

Most insects do not need to drink since they get all the water they need from their food. Witchetty grubs of Australian deserts live within the moisture-storing roots of trees. The darkling beetle of the Namib Desert has developed an amazing feat – drinking the morning mist that rolls in from the nearby sea. It stands with head down and rear end up, on the top of a sand dune, as the tiny moisture droplets float past. Condensation builds up on its shiny body and rolls down to its head, where the beetle drinks the drops.

Harvester ants
These busy insects make huge stores of seeds and other plant materials.

Witchetty grubs
There are various types of these grubs in the dry Australian outback. They grow into adult beetles or moths.

47

The Desert Sundial

There is plenty of sunshine in most deserts. You can use the Sun to tell the time and also the direction. Before people had detailed maps and satellite navigation around the globe, old-time explorers found their way by the position of the Sun, and the Moon and stars.

WARNING *Never look directly at the Sun, even with sunglasses, and especially not through a telescope or binoculars. It could damage your eyesight.*

Animals also use the Sun as a 'clock'. Some are diurnal – they wake up at sunrise and are active during daylight hours. They rest and sleep at night. We do this ourselves.

Others are nocturnal. They get up when the Sun goes down, and they are out and about during darkness. Many desert creatures are nocturnal, to take advantage of the cooler conditions at night.

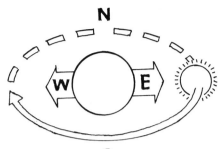

1 All over the world, the Sun rises in the east and sets in the west. So you can use it as a simple compass.

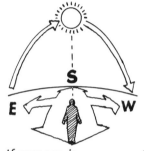

2 If you are in the northern hemisphere (top half of the world) and you face the Sun at midday, you are looking south.

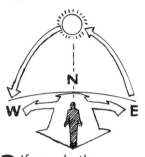

3 If you do the same as step 2, but you are in the southern hemisphere, you are facing north.

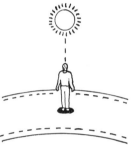

4 If the Sun is directly overhead at midday, then your desert is somewhere in the tropics. But you probably know this already!

5 To make the sundial, you need a strip of thick card, a flat piece of wood, glue and a pencil. Fold the card in half diagonally to make a double-thickness triangle.

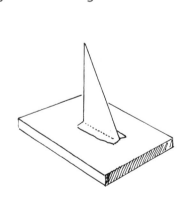

6 Fold back two strips of card along one edge of the triangle, at right angles. Glue these to the wood so that the triangle is upright.

7 Place the sundial outside on a sunny day. The triangle must line up North-South (use a compass to check this).

8 As the Sun moves across the sky, it casts a shadow of the triangle on the wooden block. Mark the shadows every hour with the pencil, using a clock or watch to tell the time.

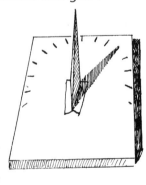

9 Next day, you can tell the time without a clock or watch, by looking at the position of the shadow on the sundial. But only if it's sunny!

Baked, Frozen and Cracked

There are huge areas of rocky deserts where the stones and pebbles are baked in the Sun by day, and become very cool at night. These changes in temperature make the rock crack and flake. Gradually, large boulders are reduced to small pebbles. The effects of frost, and the occasional flood of rushing water from a desert storm, greatly speed the process. How long does it take to crack up your own rock, by copying the desert conditions? You need the help of an adult, and the regular use of an oven or cooker and a fridge or deep-freeze.

1 Choose a suitable rock for the experiment. It should be about fist-sized or slightly smaller. It can be smooth and rounded, or sharp and angular.

2 If you can, identify the type of rock, by looking in suitable books or getting the advice of an expert. This will give a clue to its hardness. Soft rocks are best for this experiment.

3 You need to make the rock very hot, preferably once each day. Ask an adult to put it on a small metal tray in the oven or cooker, when this is being used.

4 As the rock gets hot, it expands (or gets slightly larger). When the oven goes off, ask the adult to take the rock out. Be sure to let it cool before touching it.

5 Each night, place the rock in its tray in the freezing compartment of a fridge or in the deep-freeze. It gets colder and contracts (or shrinks slightly). Take it out each morning.

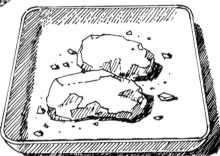

6 Every three days, soak the rock in cold water for an hour, before putting it in the cooker or freezer. This is like the soaking from a desert rainstorm.

7 After a few days or weeks of these desert-like changes in temperature, do you see any difference in the rock? The continuing expansion and contraction cause great stresses and strains, even in solid rock. Tiny cracks may appear on its surface. Pieces might even flake off into the tray.

Burrowers on Night Shift

Beneath the roasting or freezing desert surface, it is cool by day and warm at night. Inside caves, tunnels, burrows and chambers, the air stays damp. Small animals get too hot or too cold very quickly when exposed, so they live in burrows, coming out mainly at night to feed. Creatures that are out and about by night are nocturnal. They have several advantages, in addition to avoiding the extremes of temperature. In daylight, predators can easily spot scurrying animals from a great distance. Under the cover of the darkness, it is safer for small animals to move about and feed. Many night-time animals are coloured like the sand or rocks around them, for camouflage when the bright moon is shining.

Night-time animals also have extra-sharp senses. They need huge eyes to see in the darkness, a good sense of smell to find food and detect enemies, and good hearing to listen for danger. A gerbil's ears are

Day and night shift
A few animals are out and about by day in the desert. As they look for food, water and mates, nocturnal animals rest and sleep in their burrows. When dusk falls, the shift changes. The nocturnal creatures emerge and the daytime ones retire, sometimes to the same burrows. It's a simple swap system, as the day and night shifts change over.

Sand skink
This small-legged lizard 'swims' through the loose sand of its Australian desert home. It burrows in search of small creatures to eat.

Saw-scaled viper
This snake from the deserts of North Africa and Asia has the strongest poison of any viper. It moves by sideways loops, like the sidewinder rattlesnake of North American arid lands.

Desert hedgehog
Like its spiny cousins in Europe and North America, the desert hedgehog hides by day. It snuffles about at night in search of insects, worms, fruits and other foods.

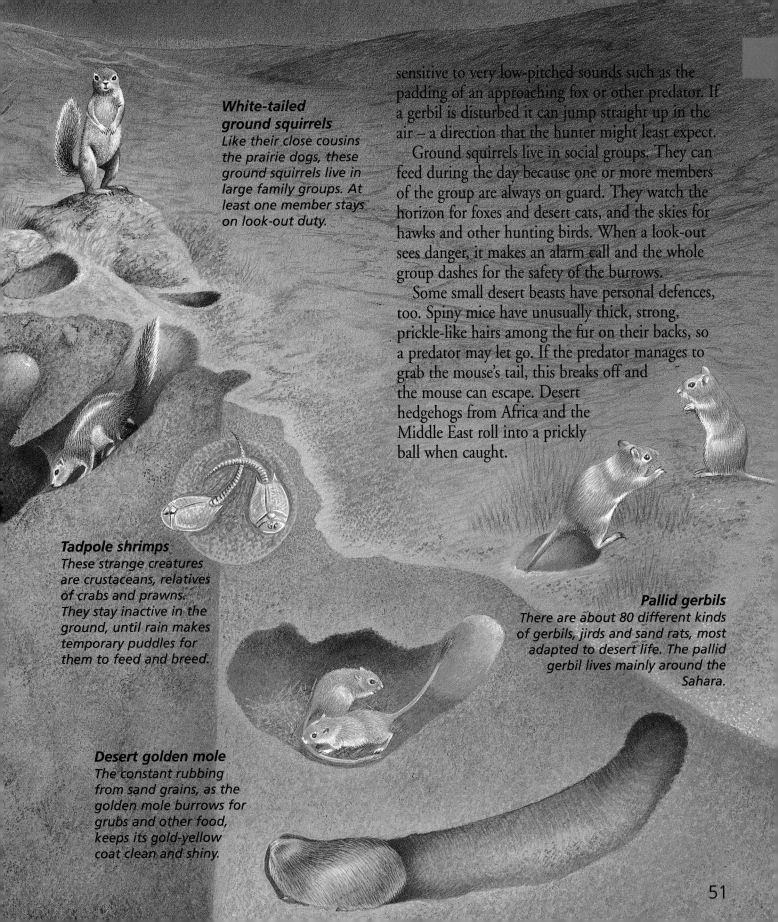

White-tailed ground squirrels
Like their close cousins the prairie dogs, these ground squirrels live in large family groups. At least one member stays on look-out duty.

sensitive to very low-pitched sounds such as the padding of an approaching fox or other predator. If a gerbil is disturbed it can jump straight up in the air – a direction that the hunter might least expect.

Ground squirrels live in social groups. They can feed during the day because one or more members of the group are always on guard. They watch the horizon for foxes and desert cats, and the skies for hawks and other hunting birds. When a look-out sees danger, it makes an alarm call and the whole group dashes for the safety of the burrows.

Some small desert beasts have personal defences, too. Spiny mice have unusually thick, strong, prickle-like hairs among the fur on their backs, so a predator may let go. If the predator manages to grab the mouse's tail, this breaks off and the mouse can escape. Desert hedgehogs from Africa and the Middle East roll into a prickly ball when caught.

Tadpole shrimps
These strange creatures are crustaceans, relatives of crabs and prawns. They stay inactive in the ground, until rain makes temporary puddles for them to feed and breed.

Pallid gerbils
There are about 80 different kinds of gerbils, jirds and sand rats, most adapted to desert life. The pallid gerbil lives mainly around the Sahara.

Desert golden mole
The constant rubbing from sand grains, as the golden mole burrows for grubs and other food, keeps its gold-yellow coat clean and shiny.

Desert Birds

Birds have several built-in advantages for desert life. They are warm-blooded and their body temperature is usually higher than the body temperature of mammals, so they are less affected by desert heat. If they become too hot, they can fly up to cooler air high above. They can also cover long distances to find water and shade. But this does not mean life is easy. Seed-eating birds need to drink daily to help them digest their dry food. In Australia, desert water-holes attract huge flocks of budgerigars in the early morning, before they fly off to search for seeds. They roost in trees during the hottest part of the day. The sandgrouse soaks its breast feathers at a water-hole. Then it flies back to the nest, where the chicks sip the moisture from the feathers.

Elf owl
One of the smallest owls, the size of your hand, the elf owl may nest in an old woodpecker hole in a giant saguaro cactus. Its main prey is large flying insects.

Roadrunner
This speedy mover of America's Sonoran and Mojave deserts is not flightless, but it usually walks or runs. It hunts insects, lizards, snakes and other creatures.

Sandgrouse
These birds soak up water in their breast feathers, to take back to their young in the nest. They eat mainly seeds and other plant material.

Budgerigar
This popular cage bird comes from the deserts and dry outback of Australia. Dense flocks of many thousands swoop and whirl in unison around water-holes and feeding areas.

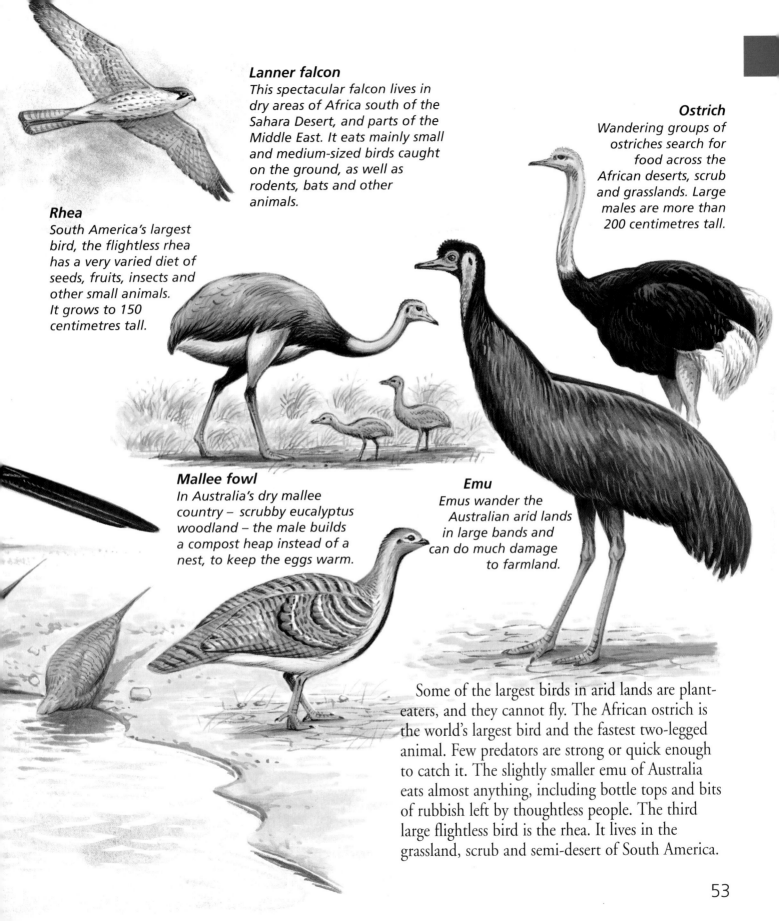

Lanner falcon
This spectacular falcon lives in dry areas of Africa south of the Sahara Desert, and parts of the Middle East. It eats mainly small and medium-sized birds caught on the ground, as well as rodents, bats and other animals.

Ostrich
Wandering groups of ostriches search for food across the African deserts, scrub and grasslands. Large males are more than 200 centimetres tall.

Rhea
South America's largest bird, the flightless rhea has a very varied diet of seeds, fruits, insects and other small animals. It grows to 150 centimetres tall.

Mallee fowl
In Australia's dry mallee country – scrubby eucalyptus woodland – the male builds a compost heap instead of a nest, to keep the eggs warm.

Emu
Emus wander the Australian arid lands in large bands and can do much damage to farmland.

Some of the largest birds in arid lands are plant-eaters, and they cannot fly. The African ostrich is the world's largest bird and the fastest two-legged animal. Few predators are strong or quick enough to catch it. The slightly smaller emu of Australia eats almost anything, including bottle tops and bits of rubbish left by thoughtless people. The third large flightless bird is the rhea. It lives in the grassland, scrub and semi-desert of South America.

Large Grazers

Being a large animal in a hot desert climate has advantages. Large bodies heat up and cool down more slowly than small bodies, so big creatures are less affected by extremes and sudden changes in temperature. Also, long legs cover the ground more quickly than short legs, to look for food and water, or to escape from enemies.

However, there are problems. Large plant-eaters like goats, camels, donkeys, gazelles and ibex cannot hide under rocks or in burrows, like smaller creatures. There are few trees for shade – so they have to stay out in the sun. The thick fur coats on their backs help to shade their skin, so that it does

Big herbivores
The wild asses of Africa and Asia live in semi-desert areas, in loose herds. The Arabian oryx survives in the most extreme desert conditions, scraping a hole in a sand dune to get shade from the sun. Dorcas gazelles are found in arid lands across North Africa and the Middle East to India.

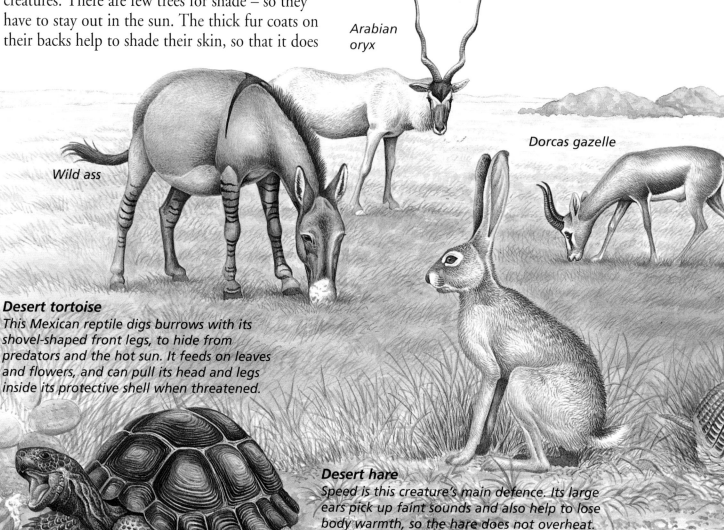

Arabian oryx

Dorcas gazelle

Wild ass

Desert tortoise
This Mexican reptile digs burrows with its shovel-shaped front legs, to hide from predators and the hot sun. It feeds on leaves and flowers, and can pull its head and legs inside its protective shell when threatened.

Desert hare
Speed is this creature's main defence. Its large ears pick up faint sounds and also help to lose body warmth, so the hare does not overheat.

not get too hot and sunburned. The fur on their undersides is much finer, so that excess body heat can be lost to the cool air in the shadows below. Donkeys use their big ears to get rid of extra heat.

Camels, donkeys and some other large desert mammals can allow their bodies to get much hotter or colder than non-desert mammals, without harm. At night the body temperature drops below normal, and by day it gradually creeps up. When the temperature reaches danger point, the animal begins to sweat and cool down – but only as a last resort, since sweating uses up body water very quickly.

In the marsupial group of mammals, the baby develops mainly in its mother's pocket-like pouch, or marsupium. Marsupials live mainly in Australia, with a few in South America, and many are adapted to desert life. The largest is the red kangaroo, standing taller than an adult human and weighing up to 70 kilograms. Red kangaroos wander the grassy plains and semi-desert scrub of central Australia, resting by day in the shade of a tree or rocky outcrop, and feeding at dusk and dawn.

Ring-tailed rock wallaby
This marsupial's feet are adapted for leaping and scrambling across the rocky outcrops and boulders of arid central and eastern Australia. Once hunted for its fine fur, it is now rare.

Red kangaroo
The male has reddish fur and is called a 'boomer'. The female is pale blue-grey and known as a 'blue flier'. Kangaroos eat grass, leaves and other plant parts.

Armadillos
They may look like scaly reptiles, but the armadillos of the Americas are furry mammals. They have horn plates in their skin for protection.

The Desert Storm

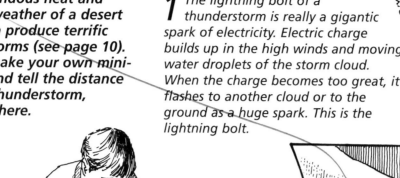

The tremendous heat and extreme weather of a desert region can produce terrific thunderstorms (see page 10). You can make your own mini-version, and tell the distance of a real thunderstorm, as shown here.

1 The lightning bolt of a thunderstorm is really a gigantic spark of electricity. Electric charge builds up in the high winds and moving water droplets of the storm cloud. When the charge becomes too great, it flashes to another cloud or to the ground as a huge spark. This is the lightning bolt.

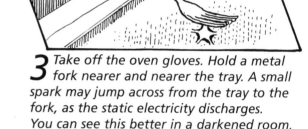

2 You can make a small, safe 'thunderflash' by placing a metal baking tray on a clean plastic dustbin-liner or rubbish bag, on a wooden table. Wearing oven gloves, rub the tray strongly to and fro across the plastic. This generates static electricity.

3 Take off the oven gloves. Hold a metal fork nearer and nearer the tray. A small spark may jump across from the tray to the fork, as the static electricity discharges. You can see this better in a darkened room.

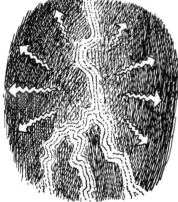

5 The light from the lightning bolt travels at the speed of light. It takes almost no time to go a few kilometres. The booming sound of thunder travels at the speed of sound. This is about 1,200 kilometres per hour or 340 metres per second.

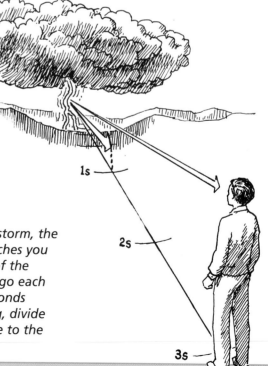

4 The real lightning spark is so incredibly hot that it makes the air next to it 'boil'. The column of air around the flash expands very fast, almost instantly. This creates the sound of the thunderclap.

6 If you experience a thunderstorm, the light from the lightning reaches you almost at once. But the sound of the thunder takes three seconds to go each kilometre. Count the gap in seconds between the flash and the bang, divide by three, and this is the distance to the storm centre, in kilometres.

Making Mirages

Mirages are caused by the refraction or bending of light. This happens as light rays go through layers of air at different temperatures. Because of the temperature differences, the layers of air are different 'thicknesses' or densities. The very hot midday air at ground level in deserts, plus the generally bare landscape, produces very clear mirages. You can see light refraction in many other places too, as shown below.

1 Look at your finger through a clear glass jamjar. See how it looks bent, or even disjointed! The light rays bend as they pass from air into the much denser glass, and they bend back again as they come out from the dense glass into the air.

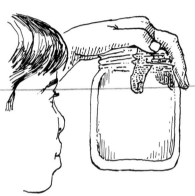

2 Part-fill the jamjar with water, and stick in your finger. See how it looks bent again. Water refracts light rays in much the same way as glass, because it is much denser than air.

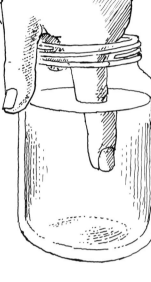

3 On a hot day, you can 'see the heat rising' from a smooth patch of ground, especially a road, car park or playground. The scene behind wobbles and wavers. This shimmering effect is also very common in the midday heat of the desert. It is due to light rays being refracted (redirected) by the different densities of hot air swirling up from the surface.

4 Sometimes on a hot day, you can see a mirage on the road. It often looks like a pool or puddle of water. When you reach the place, it's completely dry – yet again, there's a puddle in the distance. The 'water' is light rays from the sky, refracted by the hot air near the road, and bent back up into your eyes.

Desert Hunters

Desert meat-eaters, or carnivores, are not usually as specialized as the plant-eaters. Their food is mainly the flesh of other animals, and this contains lots of water in the form of blood and body fluids. So desert hunters do not need to drink extra water very often. When they do need water, and they visit an oasis or pool, other animals tend to make way for them and leave them in peace!

Also, meat-eaters need smaller amounts of food than plant-eaters, because their food is generally more nutritious. They often hunt at dawn or dusk, or during the night. Then they hide away during the hot daytime, sleeping in the shade of burrows or caves. Despite these advantages, life is never easy in the desert. Prey animals are often scarce and difficult to find, since they hide well or have good camouflage. They are also awkward to pursue and catch. So desert carnivores often have huge territories – areas of land where they live and hunt. They must defend their territories against others of their kind.

Ups and downs

When conditions are good, plants thrive. The numbers of plant-eaters such as rats, mice and gerbils go up. This means carnivores like foxes and cats have more prey, so their numbers rise too. When conditions become tough again, the reverse happens. These ups and downs are especially noticeable in the desert, where there is less variety of species, and so fewer alternative sources of food.

Population peak

Herbivore numbers

Carnivore numbers

Population crash

All amphibians – frogs, toads, newts and salamanders – are hunters. Surprisingly for these animals, which need water to breed, some kinds thrive in the desert. They include the water-holding frog of Australia and various kinds of spadefoot toad. The water-holding frog lies buried under the ground in a waterproof 'bag' or cocoon for years, until the rain soaks down into the soil and brings it to the surface. Then it feeds on the myriad insects that are also racing to reproduce in and around the pools. The amphibians lay their eggs in these temporary ponds, and the tadpoles hatch, grow and mature quickly in the warm water.

Warm-blooded hunters

Mammals use up lots of their food and energy simply staying alive and active. So there is less to pass on to the next links in the food chains. The numbers of top hunters are relatively low.

Cold-blooded hunters

Unlike mammals, insects and reptiles use little energy to stay warm. They absorb the sun's heat. More energy passes along the food chains. This makes for more top hunters in the same area of desert (see page 61).

Carnivore biomass

Herbivore biomass

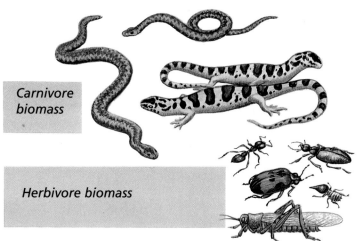

Carnivore biomass

Herbivore biomass

Small Hunters

Some of the most ferocious desert hunters are smaller than your finger. They are centipedes, insects, scorpions, spiders and other invertebrates (animals without backbones). They fight daily battles with lethal weapons and poisons to subdue and kill their victims. Most are nocturnal hunters. They hide under stones or in burrows in the heat of the day, and come out at night to search for prey.

Scorpions use their tail stings mainly for self-defence, and to kill prey. They hunt by darkness and catch insects, spiders, mice and other small rodents, and similar creatures. Like all invertebrates they are cold-blooded and inactive for much of the time. So they use little energy. This means they do not need to eat very often, and they never drink.

Locust-hunter wasp
This wasp stings and paralyzes a locust or similar creature and lays its eggs on the body, which is then buried. When the grubs hatch, they feed on the paralyzed victim.

Desert scorpion
The powerful poison is stabbed into the victim by the sharp-tipped tail sting. The scorpion tears up its prey using its strong pincers, called 'pedipalps'.

Wolf spider
Instead of making webs, these spiders hunt by stealth. They have good eyesight, and when they spot a victim, they creep towards it and pounce at the last minute. Poison is injected through two sharp fangs.

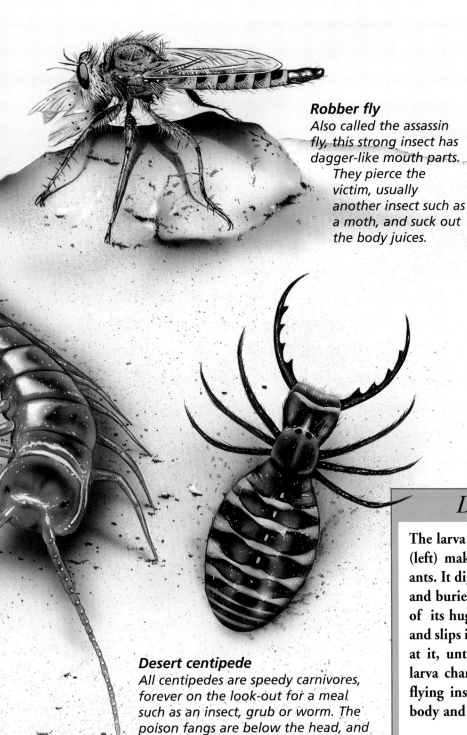

Robber fly
Also called the assassin fly, this strong insect has dagger-like mouth parts. They pierce the victim, usually another insect such as a moth, and suck out the body juices.

'Cold-blooded' means that a creature cannot make its own body heat. So its body temperature is about the same as that of the surroundings. When the conditions are cool, so are the bodies of invertebrates, which are all cold-blooded. Their body processes slow down and they cannot move very fast or be active.

'Warm-blooded' animals – like mammals and birds – make their own body heat. So they can be active at any time, even on the coldest night. But this uses a lot of energy, which must come from food (see page 59). This is why mammals and birds must eat so much, and take in more water. A cold-blooded invertebrate, like a scorpion, needs less than one-tenth the amount of food needed by the same-sized mammal or bird.

Desert centipede
All centipedes are speedy carnivores, forever on the look-out for a meal such as an insect, grub or worm. The poison fangs are below the head, and the many legs move this creature swiftly over the desert's surface.

DEATH IN THE SAND

The larva or grub of the insect called the ant-lion (left) makes a trap to catch its favourite food – ants. It digs a funnel-shaped pit in the desert sand and buries itself at the bottom, with only the tips of its huge jaws showing. When an ant stumbles and slips into the pit, the ant-lion flicks loose sand at it, until it falls into the jaws. This fearsome larva changes into the ant-lion adult, a graceful flying insect like a small damselfly, with a long body and delicately veined wings.

Reptiles in the Desert

Reptiles such as snakes and lizards are very successful desert creatures. They are cold-blooded animals, which means that they get their warmth from their surroundings. So they do not need to take in as much food or water as warm-blooded birds and mammals (see pages 59 and 61). Reptiles thrive in hot, dry places. Every morning they warm themselves in the sun, so that they can become active. They dart or slither off to hunt their prey. When they get too hot in the middle of the day, they hide in the shade. To breed, many desert reptiles simply bury their eggs in the hot sand and leave them to develop and hatch on their own.

Lizards are mainly daytime hunters. They have good eyesight and some, like chameleons, can change colour to blend in with the

Frilled lizard
This fierce-looking lizard inhabits woods and dry scrub in north Australia. When threatened, it makes the flaps of skin around its head stand out sideways, opens its mouth, and rears up on its back legs.

Thorny devil
This slow-moving Australian lizard has no need for speed – it is completely covered in sharp spines and spikes. It wanders the western deserts looking for ants and termites to eat.

Perenty
Australia's largest lizard, and the world's second largest, the perenty may reach 2.5 metres in length. It dwells in the arid central regions and can tackle prey the size of a young kangaroo.

Gila monster
This heavy-bodied reptile dwells in the dry south-western and southern North America.

Death adder
This poisonous snake comes from the outback of Australia. It is related to the cobras of Asia and the mambas of Africa.

background. Many lizards, like the bearded dragon and the thorny devil, have spiky armour plating for defence. Some can even shed their tails if they are caught. The fringe-toed lizard of North Africa has long and widely spaced toes, so it does not sink into the soft Saharan sand.

Snakes are more secretive creatures and hunt mainly at dawn and dusk, or at night. They find prey by flicking out their tongues to 'taste' the air. Sidewinders and rattlesnakes can sense the body heat of warm-blooded victims using heat-detecting pit organs just underneath their eyes. The rattlesnake kills with its poisonous fangs, but the king snake wraps itself around its victim and squeezes.

Many desert animals dig permanent burrows, but this is not possible in loose sand. The sand viper bends its body into concertina folds and then wriggles so that it sinks into the sand, leaving only its eyes and nose above the surface.

Collared lizard
These come from the dry south-west and south of North America. They can run very fast on their hind legs and they eat insects and other small lizards. Their mouths are jet-black inside.

SLIDING SIDEWAYS

Sidewinder snakes have a special way of getting across the hot sand. They throw their bodies into sideways waves so their bellies touch the ground only briefly. This prevents them from getting too hot on the scorching surface. It is also an efficient way to move over the loose grains of sand. The sidewinder leaves a series of sideways marks, like tyre or tank tracks.

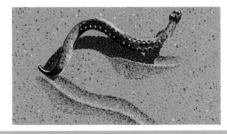

Flying Scavengers

Nothing is wasted in the desert. Any scrap of food or edible item is precious, as is every drop of water. When an animal is sick or dies, its body attracts scavengers large and small, from far and wide. The coyotes of North America are very successful at this way of life, despite the efforts of farmers over many years to kill them. Their success is partly because they will eat almost anything they can find, from berries and insects to the bodies of dead animals.

Hyenas live a similar life in the arid lands of Africa. They have the most powerful jaws of almost any animal, and they can crack the hardest bones to lick out the soft, juicy marrow. Hyenas hunt well too and, in a pack, they can tackle large victims like

Champion gliders
Hawks know where to look for the best thermals. Darker ground, such as dull-coloured rocks, heats up quickly and so has good thermals above it.

Aerial scavenging
There is a good living to be made by scavengers, such as vultures and condors. Animal deaths from thirst and heatstroke are common in the desert.

Diamondback rattlesnake
This is probably the most dangerous snake in North America. It hunts birds, small mammals and lizards in the cool of the evening and at night.

zebras and antelopes (see page 66). But if there is dead meat around, they settle for the lazy scavenging approach. Hyenas may drive a cheetah or lion from its kill and take over, or finish off the skin and bones after the big cats have had their fill.

Vultures are expert scavengers. They soar high in the sky on the rising thermals (currents) of hot air caused by the sun-heated land below. From great heights they scan the desert for signs of distress and death. When one vulture spots a carcass and starts to descend, others see it and follow, and this effect spreads across the high sky. Within minutes, various vultures appear at the carcass, as if by magic. These birds have no feathers on their heads and necks, so they can reach inside a carcass and peck off scraps of meat and gristle, without getting too messy.

Follow-my-leader
Coyotes watch the circling scavengers in the sky and follow them to the next food source. They arrive in time to get a decent meal.

Far-seeing
Keen eyesight is very important. Where you could see just a speck, a desert eagle or a vulture would see what sort of animal it is, and whether it is healthy or weak and dying.

SAND DANCERS

Many lizards are well adapted to life in the desert. Their long toes spread their weight on soft ground and let them run over very hot rocks without burning their scaly skin.

Collared lizard

65

Hunting Mammals

Carnivorous mammals of the desert usually have good eyesight to spot their prey, and they often have sandy-coloured coats for camouflage, so they can creep up on others without being seen. Many have long legs, too, for speed in such open country.

Some kinds of cats, dogs and foxes have become adapted to desert life. The caracal is a long-legged, tufted-eared cat of the deserts in Africa and the Middle East. It lives a solitary life, hunting small animals in the twilight of dawn and dusk. The wild cats that live in sandy deserts have lighter-coloured coats than their forest-dwelling cousins. Cheetahs also live in deserts and dry savannah (grassland). They can out-run most of the large day-time herbivores, like antelopes and gazelles.

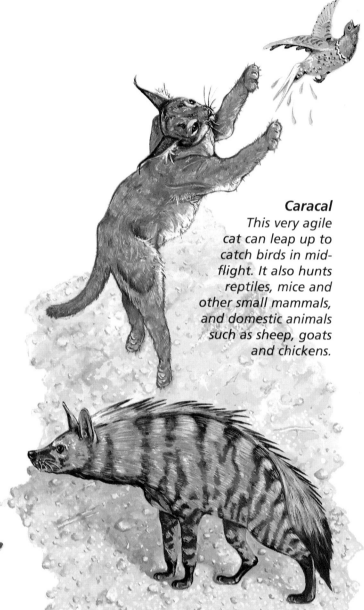

Caracal
This very agile cat can leap up to catch birds in mid-flight. It also hunts reptiles, mice and other small mammals, and domestic animals such as sheep, goats and chickens.

Fennec fox
The smallest fox, the fennec hides in a burrow by day, which it digs in the sand or loose earth. Fennecs live across North Africa and the Middle East.

Striped hyena
Hyenas are master scavengers of deserts and arid lands (see page 65). The striped hyena shown here, of Africa, the Middle East and India, tends to live on its own. Spotted hyenas live in packs of 10–30.

In Australia, the famous dog without a bark, the dingo, used to hunt small kangaroos, wallabies and other native wildlife. Now it finds that rabbits, and sometimes sheep, are easier prey. Dingoes may have come to Australia with the first Aboriginal people, over 40,000 years ago.

The tiny fennec fox of the Sahara feeds on small rodents, reptiles, insects and birds. It has huge ears which act as radiators, keeping its body cool by giving off heat to the air. These ears can also pick up a tiny sound, such as beetles scrabbling in sand.

Surviving In The Desert

Humans are not suited to desert life. The heat and lack of water can kill a person very quickly. Sun and the hot sand or rock burn skin. The endless, featureless landscape also makes it difficult to find your way.

Precautions

Never travel alone. Take someone who knows the area and the ways of the desert. Tell someone where you are going and when you will be back.

Clothing

Wear light colours that reflect the heat. Loose clothing lets cooling air circulate around the body. A large hat gives shade, and thick-soled shoes protect against hot sand and rocks, prickly plants and dangerous desert animals.

Equipment

Sunglasses cut glare and 'sand blindness'. Carry a compass, maps and plenty of water. Use this with extreme care. Plants grow where there is water, and contain water. Moisture can seep from a cut in a cactus.

Moving about

Travel in the cool of morning and evening. Try to rest in the main heat of the day, in any patch of shade. Make a shady shelter by piling up rocks or spreading a survival sheet over a bush or tree branch. If you get lost, make a large pattern in the sand or with rocks, visible from the air.

A Water Still

Even in very dry sand or soil, there is usually some moisture, which can be made to condense with a water still. It may not be plentiful or pure, but it can save life.

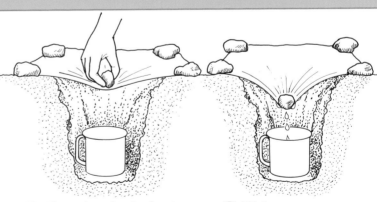

1 Dig a steep-sided hole about 60 centimetres deep and 30 across. Put a cup in the middle of the hole's bottom.

2 Place the plastic sheet over the hole, edges weighted with small boulders. Put a small pebble in the middle to form a cone, its tip just above the cup.

3 Water vapour seeps from the soil into the air in the hole. It slowly condenses into water on the plastic sheet and then drips into the cup.

Amazing Facts

About one-third of the Earth's land surface is arid.

- *1 per cent is extremely arid with almost no rain*
- *16.5 per cent is arid where farming is only possible with irrigation*
- *17.5 per cent is semi-arid where farming is possible on a seasonal basis.*

Only one-third of the world's deserts are sand-covered.

The Gobi Desert is the least populated area in the world, apart from the ice caps at the poles.

It is estimated that every year, 12 million hectares of arid lands around the edges of natural deserts, themselves turn into desert. This process, desertification, is due mainly to over-grazing by farm animals and general poor farming methods.

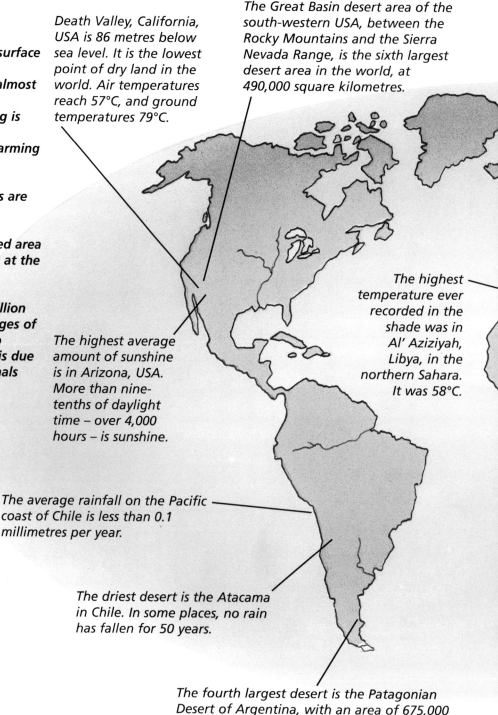

Death Valley, California, USA is 86 metres below sea level. It is the lowest point of dry land in the world. Air temperatures reach 57°C, and ground temperatures 79°C.

The Great Basin desert area of the south-western USA, between the Rocky Mountains and the Sierra Nevada Range, is the sixth largest desert area in the world, at 490,000 square kilometres.

The highest temperature ever recorded in the shade was in Al' Aziziyah, Libya, in the northern Sahara. It was 58°C.

The highest average amount of sunshine is in Arizona, USA. More than nine-tenths of daylight time – over 4,000 hours – is sunshine.

The average rainfall on the Pacific coast of Chile is less than 0.1 millimetres per year.

The driest desert is the Atacama in Chile. In some places, no rain has fallen for 50 years.

The fourth largest desert is the Patagonian Desert of Argentina, with an area of 675,000 square kilometres, over two and a half times the size of Britain.

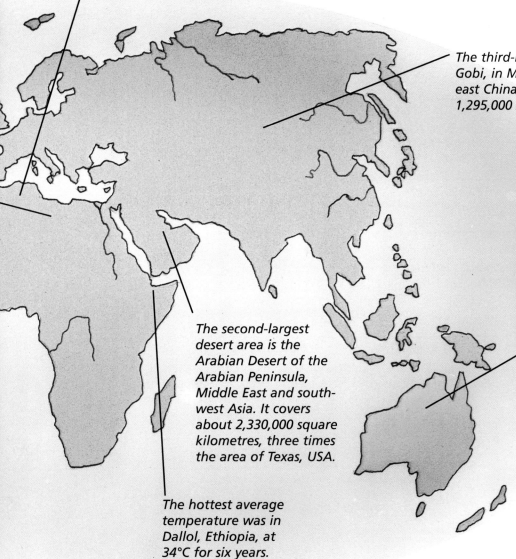

The largest sand dunes in the world are in the Sahara in Algeria. They have a wavelength (peak to peak distance) of 5 kilometres and some are almost 500 metres high.

The third-largest desert is the Gobi, in Mongolia and north-east China. It covers around 1,295,000 square kilometres.

At Marble Bar, Australia, the maximum temperature reaches 49°C. It was more than 38°C for 162 days, the longest sustained high temperatures anywhere in the world.

The second-largest desert area is the Arabian Desert of the Arabian Peninsula, Middle East and south-west Asia. It covers about 2,330,000 square kilometres, three times the area of Texas, USA.

The hottest average temperature was in Dallol, Ethiopia, at 34°C for six years.

The largest desert is the Sahara, with an area of 5,600,000 square kilometres. Its maximum measurements are 5,105 kilometres east to west and 2,250 kilometres north to south. Temperatures can vary between 52.2°C at midday to –3.3°C the following night.

Australia has more desert, compared to its total land area, than any other continent. More than two-thirds of its 7,682,300 square kilometres is arid or semi-arid.
The Great Victoria Desert is the biggest of Australia's desert areas and the world's fifth-largest desert, at 650,000 square kilometres.

Find Out More

There are no true deserts or even semi-deserts in Britain. But there are various places where water is lacking, because it rains infrequently and/or the water drains away quickly. These include steep hill slopes with sandy soil, sand heaths, the sandy or gravelly sides to lakes and rivers, and sand or shingle beaches and dunes.

Visit these dry places to get some idea of the problems faced by their wildlife. The best organization to start with is your local County Wildlife Trust. This has details of habitats, plants and animals in your area. Ask at your library or contact The Wildlife Trusts (see General Information).

GENERAL INFORMATION

Arid Lands Initiative, Machpelah Works, Burnley Road, Hebden Bridge HX7 7AV, 01422 843807

Council for the Protection of Rural England, 25 Buckingham Palace Rd, London SW1W 0PP, 0171–976 6433

Countryside Commission, John Dower House, Crescent Place, Cheltenham, Glos GL50 3RA, 01242 521381

English Nature, Northminster House, Peterborough, Cambs PE1 1UA, 01733 340345

Geological Society, Burlington House, Piccadilly, London W1V 0JU, 0171–434 9944

Institute of Estuarine and Coastal Studies, University of Hull, Cottingham Rd, Hull, Humberside HU6 7RX, 01482 46311 ext 7511

Institute of Terrestrial Ecology, 68 Hills Road, Cambridge CB2 1LA, 01223 69745

National Trust for Scotland, 5 Charlotte Square, Edinburgh EH2 4DU, 0131–226 5922

National Trust, 42 Queen Anne's Gate, London SW1H 9AS, 0171–222 9251

Open Spaces Society, 25a Bell Street, Henley-on-Thames, Oxon RG9 2BA, 014912 573535

Ramblers' Association, 1-5 Wandsworth Rd, London SW8 2XX, 0171–582 6878

Royal Botanic Gardens, Kew, Richmond, Surrey TW9 3AB, 0181–940 1171

Soil Association Ltd, 86-88 Colston Street, Bristol BS1 5BB, 01272 290661

The Wildlife Trusts, The Green, Witham Park, Waterside South, Lincoln LN5 7JR, 01522 544400

Zoological Society of London, Regent's Park, London NW1 4RY, 0171–722 3333

LEARNING ABOUT NATURE

Amateur Entomologists' Society, 355 Hounslow Rd, Hanworth, Feltham, Middx TW13 5JL, 0181–755 0325

Botanical Society of the British Isles, c/o Department of Botany, Natural History Museum, Cromwell Road, London, SW7 5BD, 0171–938 9026

British Naturalists' Association, 1 Bracken Mews, Chingford, London E4 7UT

Fauna and Flora Preservation Society, 1 Kensington Gore, London, SW7 2AR, 0171–823 8899

Field Studies Council, Preston Montford, Montford Bridge, Shrewsbury SY4 1HW, 01743 850674

Royal Society for the Protection of Birds (RSPB), The Lodge, Sandy, Bedfordshire SG19 2DL, 01767 680551

HOW CAN I HELP?

British Trust for Conservation Volunteers 36 St Mary's Street, Wallingford, Oxon OX10 0EU, 01491 39766

Friends of the Earth, 26–28 Underwood St, London N1 7JQ, 0171–490 1555

Greenpeace UK, Canonbury Villas, London N1 2PN, 0171–354 5100

Wildlife Watch Trust for Environmental Education, The Green, Witham Park, Waterside South, Lincoln LN5 7JR, 01522 544400

Worldwide Fund for Nature (WWF), Panda House, Weyside Park, Godalming, Surrey GU7 1XR, 01483 426444

BOOKS

The Amateur Naturalist Gerald Durrell, Penguin

Atlas of Endangered Species editor John Burton, Macmillan, 1991

Deserts and Wastelands Watts Picture Atlas series

Eyewitness Guides – Desert Dorling Kindersley

Junior Nature Guides series Dragon's World Children's Books 1993–95

Nature Atlas of Great Britain Pan / Ordnance Survey, 1989

Private Life of Plants David Attenborough, BBC Enterprises, 1995

VIDEOS

The National Geographical Society and The Reader's Digest both produce a wide range of wildlife and geographical videos.

BBC Natural History produces a wide range of wildlife and geographical videos, for example *David Attenborough's World of Wildlife.*

MULTIMEDIA

3D Atlas Electronic Arts, 01753 549442

A World Alive Softline, 0181–401 1234

Eyewitness Encyclopedia of Nature Dorling Kindersley, 0171–753 3488

Global Learning Mindscape, 01444 246333

Picture Atlas of the World National Geographic Society, 01483 33161

The Big Green Disk Gale Research, 01252 737630

The Environment: Land and Air Academy Television, 01532 461528

The Image of the World British Library, 0171–636 1544

Glossary

aestivation When an animal survives hot, dry periods by becoming very inactive, as though in a deep sleep.

aquifer Rocks that contain water, usually because they are spongy.

arid Dry.

bedrock The hard, solid rock that lies below soil and looser or softer rocks.

biomass The weight of living and ex-living matter, including the plants and animals which are alive, plus their shed parts such as leaves and droppings, plus remains of animals and plants that have died and rotted.

carnivore An animal that eats other animals, usually a hunter that feeds on meat or flesh.

cold-blooded When an animal cannot generate much of its own internal warmth, so its body temperature varies with the temperature of its surroundings. The main cold-blooded animal groups are fish, amphibians, reptiles and all invertebrates. Compare WARM-BLOODED.

desert Any land where the plant cover is too low to support human life. This is currently about 33 per cent of the Earth.

desertification The creation of new deserts and dry areas from moister or damper lands, by human activities like farming or draining away water.

dormancy When a living thing remains still and inactive, as though asleep, to save energy and survive bad conditions. AESTIVATION and HIBERNATION are types of dormancy.

erosion Wearing away the land by physical methods such as rubbing and scraping, and carrying away the eroded results such as rock particles.

evaporation When a liquid turns into a vapour or gas. Liquid water evaporates or 'dries' into invisible water vapour.

food chain A list or sequence of who eats what, beginning with plants and ending with the top carnivore. In nature, many food chains usually link to form food webs.

groundwater Water under the ground, in spongy rocks and in cracks, crevices, caves and tunnels.

habitat A type of place or surroundings in the natural world, often named after the main plants that grow there. Examples are a conifer forest, a grassland such as a meadow, a heathland, a pond or a sandy seashore. Some animals are adapted to only one habitat, like limpets on rocky seashores. Other animals, like foxes, can survive in many habitats.

herbivore An animal that eats plant food, such as shoots, stems, leaves, buds, flowers and fruits.

hibernation When an animal survives cold periods by becoming very inactive, as though in a deep sleep.

oasis (pl. **oases**) a fertile area in a desert where GROUNDWATER can reach the surface because of the rock formations.

photosynthesis 'Building with light', catching the energy in sunlight and converting it into the energy in foods and nutrients, for living and growing. Plants are the main living things that photosynthesize.

precipitation The overall name for water reaching the surface of the Earth, which includes rain, sleet, snow, frost and dew.

warm-blooded When an animal can generate its own internal warmth, so its body temperature is independent of the temperature of its surroundings. The main warm-blooded animal groups are mammals and birds. Compare COLD-BLOODED.

Index

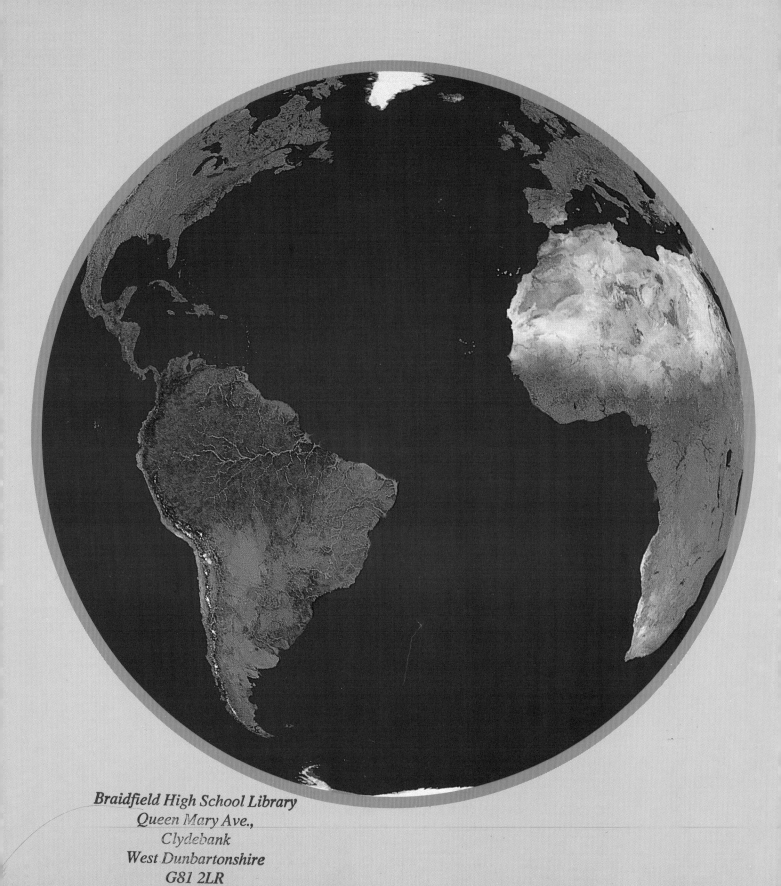